The MUSICIAN HEALER

ALSO BY ISLENE RUNNINGDEER

Musical Encounters with Dying

Stories and Lessons

Jessica Kingsley Publishers, 2013

The MUSICIAN HEALER

Transforming Art into Medicine

Islene Runningdeer

Foreword by Tanya Maggi

Calgary, Alberta, Canada

Durvile & UpRoute Books
UPROUTE IMPRINT OF DURVILE PUBLICATIONS LTD.

Calgary, Alberta, Canada
Durvile.com

LIBRARY AND ARCHIVES CATALOGUING IN PUBLICATIONS DATA

The Musician Healer: Transforming Art into Medicine
Runningdeer, Islene, author
Maggi, Tanya, foreword

1. Health Care Issues
2. Music | 3. Music Therapy | 4. Alternative Medicine

Every River Lit Series. Series editor, Lorene Shyba

978-1-988824-86-4 (pbk)
978-1-988824-98-7 (ebook)
978-1-988824-99-4 (audiobook)

Front cover painting by Mary Jo Fulmer. Illustrations by Rich Théroux.

Durvile Publications would like to acknowledge the financial support of the Government of Canada through the Canadian Heritage Canada Book Fund and the Government of Alberta, Alberta Media Fund.
Printed in Canada. First edition, first printing. 2022.

Durvile Publications recognizes the traditional territories upon which our studios rest.
The Indigenous Peoples of Southern Alberta include the
Siksika, Piikani, and Kainai of the Blackfoot Confederacy; the Dene Tsuut'ina;
the Chiniki, Bearspaw, and Wesley Stoney Nakoda First Nations;
and the Region 3 Métis Nation of Alberta.

For Livee True

Bright shining star

My beloved granddaughter

CONTENTS

CONTENTS

FOREWORD

YOU COULD HAVE HEARD A PIN DROP in the classroom the day that Islene Runningdeer came to speak to my students about death and dying. The class was riveted as she described her journey from music student sitting in the very same classroom, to Musician Healer singing with a dying man's last breath. A few students looked uncomfortable at first, some were slightly shaken, but then the room relaxed as Islene wove her magic, bringing with her words a sense of curiosity and wonder at the possibility of a musical path that stretched the imagination. By the end of class, some tears were shed, some points were made, some questions were asked, and there was no doubt that the students were changed.

I write this foreword through the eyes of a teacher, arts educator, administrator, and mentor at one of the oldest continuously operating schools of music in the United States . Every day, I work with young adult musicians who are striving to perfect their craft, a road that many of them began as early as memory stretches. We often categorize musicians like these as single minded in their drive to reach the version of success that we– their teachers, their parents, society, the field of music– have defined for them. I see something very different. I see young people who are desperate to make an impact in the world and to know that music matters. They are hungry to believe that the hours in a practice room can translate into tears of joyful recognition in a person living with dementia, or a newly composed song, written through means of deep empathy and collaboration, can ease the passage for another human being from this world. I see a fire in the belly in this next generation of musicians, now more than ever, for music to heal and to have meaning.

Our world, as Islene puts it "aches for healing."
She asks us to lend our artful expression,
coupled with healing energy,
to an ailing and needy world.

This book you hold in your hand is a window into the possibility of that meaning. Islene gives us readers not only the opportunity to learn from and alongside her experiences, but to translate them into the fabric of our own story. "I hope you will indulge me, and read this book in a thoughtful, questing way" she says, and we readers are challenged to broaden our view.

Islene's voice is one of an artful and empathetic storyteller (who also leaves room for the fun) as she carries us openly and honestly through her personal life journey, through healing wisdom from times and cultures past, through the many stories of musical healing made manifest for herself, and others. Through it all, we are continually encouraged to embrace creative imagination as we redefine what it means for every one of us to be a Musician Healer.

Our world, as Islene puts it "aches for healing." She asks us to lend our artful expression, coupled with healing energy, to an ailing and needy world. Found in these pages before you is an invitation to answer that call. I know I take away inspirational awakening and a quest to more deeply engage with my own narrative as the many facets of my musical life continue to unfold.

With that, I wish you a joyful reading journey ahead. May it take you somewhere new and uniquely be your own.

— *Tanya Maggi, Dean of Community Engagement and Professional Studies, New England Conservatory, Boston, Massachusetts*, 2022

PART ONE

ORIGINS & INSPIRATIONS

Julia Blake Lashua
My great-great grandmother.

INTRODUCTION, PART ONE

EMERGENCE OF A MUSICIAN HEALER

When I was a child, I heard stories told by my father and his sister about an Indigenous woman who, a few generations earlier, was part of our family, my great-great grandmother. They said her name was Julia Blake Lashua, sometimes called Jewel. My aunt said she was Mohegan. My dad thought Mohawk. Perhaps neither of them knew for sure. I have an old wrinkled black-and-white photo of her on my dresser wearing a simple calico house dress, her braided hair pinned to her head, standing in front of the old house in Ashburnham, Massachusetts where Dad and Aunt Dottie remembered visiting as kids. In the photo she looks a bit scary, a scowl on her face, her prominent nose aligning her head. Maybe not so much scary as hardened, revealing that she had lived through a lot of difficult stuff. I learned that her mother may well have been a full-blooded Indigenous woman, most likely from Trois-Rivières, Quebec, where my French ancestors, those who initially settled the first French colony in North America, married Indigenous women they encountered in the New World, needing companions and helpmates while they farmed or trapped or otherwise procured animal furs.

I felt my Indigenous roots early in life because of sketchy stories and an old photograph. Jewel is somewhere back there in my ancestral past, but I feel her reemerging now to guide me through another look at that vein in my soul. A piece of my origins. She urges me to finally tell the whole story of my lifelong tracing of those roots. So I will try.

My Spirit Name

When I was in my early twenties, I received my spirit name, Runningdeer—given from the Spirit World, telepathically, by an old Grandmother, as my true name. This was during difficult times as a very young single mother, a time when I was just beginning to learn about myself. I wonder if the name was bestowed by Ah Weh Eyu (Pretty Flower), an Indigenous Elder who appeared in my meditations at the time. Perhaps, or not. No matter. It was my name; and it had arrived just after I had shape-shifted into a frightened, fleeing deer in the woods, during my morning prayer walk, spooked by some unseen but felt danger. I took and wore the name and became more myself.

Several years later, I composed music to a dance-and-poetry performance piece titled "Three Origins." You will read about this later in the book, but for now I'll simply say that one of those origin pieces was simple and rhythmic, echoing the sounds and music of North American Indigenous culture. Just months before creating this music, I had ingested the psychotropic magic mushroom and spent a long night with my Indigenous woman self, growing from youth into young womanhood and on into maturity and Eldership. It was during that vision, full of color and emotion and power, that I relived my return, alone on horseback, to my burnt-out village and the ashes of all my beloveds:

I see the wide, empty plain
My people are dead
My people are dead
I hear the cold, even wind
My people are dead
My people are dead

I suspect, and still maintain, that I was that Indigenous woman in another lifetime. From that time on I have incorporated her life into my conscious self. I recognize her deep grief, which echoes from the past whenever loss crosses my path in this lifetime.

My name, Islene Runningdeer, does not appear on the official rolls of any First Nation of North America. But my identity is rooted somehow in the rhythms of Indigenous culture. I love the natural world in a way that feels ancient. I trust my deep inner acknowledgment of a healing capacity that also feels ancient and rooted in the Indigenous way of knowledge. I have endured my share of pain, both physical and psychic, in this lifetime. Perhaps my ability to suffer and rise again was injected into my soul from this connection with those people who have endured much, and still remain. Though my work as Musician Healer has been nourished by many sources, my Indigenous ancestors are an essential cadre of great support in this endeavor. I give them great thanks.

My sister researches our family genealogy and has data about the several Indigenous bloodlines that flow into the mix: Mi'kmaq, Huron, and Abenaki, all Northeast First Nations that intermingled with French settlers from the 1500s on. My mother's ancestor, Chief Henri Membertou (born early in the 1500s), was a Mi'kmaq/Meti sachem (sakmow) and healer, who led his people during the earliest arrival of French settlers at Port-Royal, present-day Nova Scotia. Chief Henri Membertou married a Mi'kmaq woman, whose Mi'kmaq name is unknown. Chief Henri Membertou was his French-given name but his First Nations People knew him as Anli-Maopeltoog (Mawpiltu). He was my tenth great-grandfather. Membertou established close relations with the French, eventually adopting their Christian Catholic religion, while maintaining his Indigenous spirituality. At the end of his life, he was baptized, given the French name Henri, and was buried in a Catholic cemetery in 1611. It is recorded that he was conflicted about this decision. I am happy to know that he was. Remarkably, he was said to be very old, possibly 104 years.

Chief Membertou left us three songs, transcribed by Marc Lescarbot, a French lawyer who met the Chief during a year-long stay in the new settlement. I have copies of this music in my personal library, which I sing and play on the piano and recorder, as a substitute for Native flute. Membertou, a great chief, was also a healer, and I imagine him singing his songs to the sick and

Engraving of Chief Henri Membertou (Mawpiltu) as seen memorialized on a Canadian postage stamp.

dying while caring for them. His spirit has been present, no doubt, as I have done the same countless times.

My father's bloodline goes all the way back to Roch Manitouabeouich, Huron, born 1596. His name meant "Resembling the Creator." His young adult life was spent as a trail guide and interpreter for Olivier Letardif, a French entrepreneur advancing the fur trade as personal representative and interpreter for Samuel De Champlain. He later settled in present-day Quebec, at the Sillery Settlement. Roch was married to Outchibahabanouk Oueou, Abenaki. Like Membertou, their descendants married French settlers, and his first child Marie's marriage to a French settler is claimed to be the first-documented mixed marriage in the New World (1644).

Abenaki woman and man, circa sixteenth century.
from the Montréal Archives, (Collection Philéas Gagnon.)

The Indigenous bloodlines go way back in my family. But Julia Blake Lashua, the woman with the worn face and the calico dress, my great-great-grandmother from more recent times, still remains a mystery. She and her mother Fanny *(b. 1850 and 1808)* were born near Trois-Rivières, Quebec, a place which was, and still is, a blend of Indigenous and French coupling. I suspect the stories I heard as a child were true, and she was an Indigenous woman. My sister and I will keep digging.

The most surprising discovery has been a link between one of Manitouabeouich's earlier French/Indigenous descendants and a bloodline that goes all the way back to 540 BCE in Egypt. I mention this, distant as it is, because of a life-long fascination I've had with ancient Egypt and all the mysteries embedded in that culture. It must have begun when my father gave me a lovely scarab bracelet when I was a teen, my first encounter with the Sacred Beetle, preserved in very ancient Egyptian iconography. My Dad had no idea that his family had deep roots in Syria, Macedonia, and Egypt, and that a woman named Cleopatra Gygaea was his ninety-seventh great-grandmother. It is amazing that, because she was of royal heritage, records still exist of all her descendants, all the way down to him and me.

The Origins of My Work

In the pages that follow in this book, you will read about four important origins that feed my profession as Musician Healer: North American First Nations, French, Indian, and Ancient Egyptian. All inform my creative inspiration. All are in my soul. All are in my work.

I hope this book will inspire you to amplify the power of your music-making with the potential to heal, to soothe, to awaken, to deeply move, and to spiritualize the experience of listening. It may even direct you to create unconventional musical work for yourself, as I have done. The most beautiful music we make becomes even more beautiful when it helps others. In this way, we become Musician Healers.

Some of the characters in the Egyptian, Seneca and Cluny stories in this book are fictitious. The names and personalities came to me through my dreams and imagination; however their stories are based on information about their times and practices, derived from scholarly research cited in the bibliography.

May my way of blending musical expression with service be a legacy to the young musicians who are considering how their music-making might meaningfully relate to a life's work. I hope you will indulge me a great favor, and read this book in a thoughtful, questing way. Perhaps something new and useful will be revealed.

— Islene Runningdeer,
Vermont, USA, 2022

ONE

CREATURES OF EXPRESSION

"We are creatures of expression."

— Islene Runningdeer

"I slept and dreamed that life was joy.
I awoke and found that life is but service.
I served and discovered that service was joy."

—Rabindranath Tagore

I HAVE BEEN a musician all my life. It is my great good fortune to have this wondrous way of expression as a constant companion. I am grateful beyond words for the joy the making of music has brought to me.

But I discovered along the way that, while I've been granted a special talent of expression via music, it should not be for my benefit and joy alone. Some wise teachers convinced me that sharing this beauty was my duty, debt, the best way I could celebrate my joy and share the wealth.

I have done my fair-share of joyful performing through the years, however, my music-making has evolved into a specific service to others. My music reaches many different kinds of people, but always with the intention of transmitting a healing balm through musical expression and the energies I cultivate and bring to bear. I've discovered that serving others in this way brings double joy. What could be better?

Much has been written in recent years about the powers of music and sound. This book is different because it focuses on the deliverer of this wonderful art form, the musician herself. The inner powers of the messenger have been forgotten over a long history, so the healing potential of music has been restrained.

It is a time when
sound, frequency, vibration, and energy
are emerging as a leading edge of
advancement in medicine and healing.

It's time for us to revive these inner powers in our new world, which aches for healing. It's also a time when sound, frequency, vibration, and energy are emerging as a leading edge of advancement in medicine and healing. All the more reason why musicians who want to make a positive difference should be considering how to best use their expressive art and energies to bring solace and balm to the world.

Developing Inner Resources

This book is for musicians, although I expect anyone interested in energy medicine will find something of value in these pages. It explores very specific ways we musical humans can develop inner resources—physical, psychological, and spiritual—in order to amplify the healing power of the music we deliver. The ideas for this book sprouted and grew as a result of conversations I had years ago with faculty, administrators, and students at the New England Conservatory of Music in Boston, my long-ago alma mater. After guest teaching a class about making-music in service to others, and generating some excitement among young, serious student musicians about the potential for beautiful music to heal in various ways, I realized that even the most prestigious temples of music education had ignored this most important potential. The ancient art of healing with music had been buried in the dust of history, to be forgotten, ridiculed, or dismissed as primitive nonsense. Fortunately, some of us have remembered and realized the potency of the music we make and have figured out ways to bring our artful expression, coupled with healing energy, to an ailing and needy world.

Student musicians are conventionally taught technique, interpretation, and performance. They are trained to be teachers of music. Composition and conducting are musical specialties which some pursue. All such education often leads to either life-long employment, or at least a life-long avocation of enjoyment and fulfillment. All wonderful outcomes. But something huge and very important is missed if musicians have not spent time understanding how their musical energy affects those who are listening. And beyond that, how we music makers can learn to generate high-quality energy from our centers and deliver it via music with healing effect. This certainly opens up a whole new venue for our art.

I have successfully brought this way of sharing music to people in hospitals, hospices, nursing homes, dementia care facilities, churches, students, and yes, even conventional audiences in music halls for many years now. It has been a long work in progress, but its positive and powerful effects have been witnessed many times over. Now that I am an Elder, it's time I share what I've learned and what I know with younger musicians so that they might pick up the ancient torch, make it new, and carry it on.

My Musical Story

I came into this world with an already-established sensitivity to sound and music and other things beautiful. It's hard to recall my very first memory of a musical experience but I can recollect both my grandmother and my mother singing to me when I was an infant. My mother had a very soothing, sweet voice, a high alto— a natural singer. My young father doodled on his clarinet, and Mom always had an old upright or spinet piano to play. My childhood home was very noisy, but in a lot of good ways. Music was always at the heart of our home life, chaotic and difficult as it sometimes was. Every one of us made and listened to music, sometimes created and enjoyed it together, other times going our own ways. I would have been lost without the deep strength of music in my early life.

I am the oldest child of my birth family, the achiever, the resilient caretaker. Four other children followed me, each with a musical gift. Singers all, instrumentalists on piano, guitar, mandolin, and trombone too. Rock 'n' roll, jazz, and classical music were just different languages each of us chose. My father wrote -era popular songs. My mother played piano works of Debussy, Gershwin, and many others from an eclectic mix. Aunts and uncles sometimes added their voices to family music fests. It was almost impossible to find privacy or peace and quiet in our family home. There was never a dull moment. It would take many decades of living to finally get to peace and quiet (and a room of one's own) in my life.

My two brothers, two sisters and I had a pretty disruptive and emotionally difficult childhood. We were loved, for sure, especially by our mother. I do believe our father loved us too but he was a troubled man who made some hard choices that affected us all deeply. When he left our family, I think I was around 11 or 12, maybe as young as 10. Of course, the process of family disintegration took a while to play out before he finally left, so I don't remember too many happy early years. My father's leaving came as a great shock and burden to my mother, who couldn't bear the emotional stress she was suffering. So, she plunged deeply into a depression that kept her in bed, in a darkened room, for I'm not certain how long.

It felt like it took a long time for her to get back on her feet and to get on with her life as our mother, a single parent, not of her own choosing. In the meanwhile, I took on family responsibilities without thinking really. It was my 'first child' automatic response to crisis, and my defensive reaction to family instability. *I can make this right,* I must have desperately believed.

I carried a lot on my shoulders at a very young age, as many firstborns do. It strengthened me, yes, but also took away a big part of my childhood. I never really felt carefree beyond a very young age. I studied hard, tried to keep things together at home as best I could from the age of 11 and on through high school—all at a great psychological cost, I eventually came to understand. Taking care of others at a time when I needed to be taken care of myself made for a flimsy foundation upon which to stand throughout my young adulthood. But through those hard years of adolescence with my birth family, music buoyed me and my spirits in a way that nothing else could.

Musical threads

Music at school was very important to me. I sang in the elite choirs and choruses, was assigned many solos and lead parts in musicals, and simply loved learning about and making music with my voice. I played the piano as well. But I didn't really find a more serious way into the wonders of that instrument until I was in my thirties. So that's for later in this story. Simply put, I loved to sing as a young girl. Without a doubt, it was my greatest joy and solace. It was the place that I could call my own, a safe place away from the troubles of my family life and the ordinary pressures of growing up.

I had heard so much music at home, classical and jazz records, and live music played by everyone in the family, that my ear was very well attuned. It's remarkable to me that today, when I sing some of the old American standards from the 1920s, '30s, and '40s to the Elders at the nursing homes where I work. I can still hear them as I heard them at home when I was growing up in the 1950s. My parents' music really nourished all of us kids. We all sang in harmony, and learning music came easily to us. Our shared music made long drives in the car such fun. We five kids filled up the back of the station wagon and sang our hearts out with my Aunt Dottie and Mother leading in front. The car must have vibrated with the two- and three-part harmonies we configured on "In the Evening by the Moonlight," "The Violins Ringing (Orchestra Song)," "Daisy," and other songs now lost to memory.

I learned then that music was fun, music felt good, music made me happy. This should be the birthright of all children. My brothers and sisters and I were really infused with a great thing, a love of the beauty of sound. So, as I draw a darker picture of a difficult childhood emotionally, which each of us did suffer, I came to realize how the healing power of music was ever present in helping us get through life. It still does. Such fortune we were bequeathed by a long family line of music lovers, it turns out. My mother's French-Canadian family was sprinkled with talented musicians: fiddlers, organists, drummers, and si ngers. My father's mother sang in nightclubs in Lowell, Massachusetts in the 1930s. I know little about the musical lives of my ancestors further back, but I suspect I would find it there too.

The musical thread follows through into my descendants as well. My adult daughter is a singer and actor. Her teenage daughter, my dear granddaughter, is both musical and theatrical. She easily takes to dancing, acting, costume play, and music. I find the thread also appearing in the children of some of my sisters and brothers. An artistic streak flows through my family lines, which is key to why music is central to my life and work. Exposure to music in the childhood home is the best way to start developing a child's musical instincts. Without having early musical experiences, a lot of good nourishment is lost to a growing person. Engagement with music makes people healthier. This is a simple truth.

Conservatory days

After high school, I went off to Boston for my freshman year at the New England Conservatory of Music (NEC). No one before me in my family had attended college, much less a prestigious music conservatory. But a dear music teacher and mentor of mine recognized a gift in me and guided me through the process of auditioning for music schools. There was no question that I would go to college; I was an exceptional academic student from a small community forty miles west of Boston. But my knowledge of Boston and city life was limited to occasional school field trips, sometimes a family trip to see the *Ice Capades*, or a Christmas concert at Boston Common. The shift from small-town to big city life would prove to be a challenge that I was not prepared for.

At 18, there were a lot of things beyond my control. I hadn't a clue as to what I might do with my life. Music seemed like the right thing, for sure. And I just happened to be talented and smart enough to get into a fine school of music. But I was so young, inexperienced, and without any sense of self-direction. I was also emotionally dependent on a relationship with a high school beau for whatever sense of emotional security my familiar attachment to him could provide. And I'd never given any thought, at that point, to what I might need to do to heal from my broken family experience and the loss of stability as a youngster. That would come much later, but for now I went along with the plan set for me by others.

The expectation of the circle of adults around me seemed to be that I would graduate after four years at NEC and then perform. You see, the adults in my life, whether close to me or not, saw a future for me that was limited by their own projected dreams and longings. But, in a wonderful and mysterious way, what ended up happening to me, and inside me, while I completed my one and only year in Boston, was the best thing that could have happened. As it turned out, my brief sojourn in the city presented a 'monumental and crucial experience', which was the beginning of a long road of discovering my true mission as a musician—that of a Musician Healer.

Before I tell you about that momentous and crucial experience, I want to share how grateful I am, and was even then, for some incredibly special musical adventures while a student at NEC. Twelve months of classroom learning, rehearsals, multiple performances in chorus with The Boston Symphony Orchestra (BSO), recording sessions with RCA Victor in Symphony Hall, concerts at Carnegie Hall with the BSO; all these riches were mine. I learned compelling and beautiful music: Ives, Copland, Britton, Mahler. I worked with some fine conductors: Lorna Cook DeVaron, Erik

Leinsdorf, and Gunther Schuller. It was a thrill to work with such fine musicians. It taught me a great deal and propelled me onto the next level of musical understanding. I still recall the careful detailed molding of voice parts which choral conductor DeVaron modeled for us young singers, and how all those details of phrase and nuance came together to create a wondrous whole. I began to learn how to really listen to internal parts, to open up a new channel in my ears. I also left with some strong skills, especially in sight-reading, both vocal and on piano. But from my current perspective, much later in life, I see now that was just the beginning of many more years of further musical training and study, albeit a most important one.

The Momentous and Crucial Experience

Let's get back to the momentous and crucial experience, which climaxed my year of study in Boston. As my freshman year neared its close, I prepared for my final voice jury, the equivalent of a final exam in one's major instrument. Little did I realize at the time that this experience would ignite the most important learning of my sojourn in the city. Memories of highly charged emotional experiences live with us throughout our years. Though this experience happened over five decades ago when I was 18, the scene remains vivid in my mind and heart.

It was a late spring morning in Boston. I'd been preparing three songs for this occasion for many weeks, but I still felt nervous waiting backstage for the announcement of my name. My accompanist and I walked out to center stage, and I immediately noticed three shaded figures sitting in the darkened hall with pads and pens in hand. The rest of the hall was empty.

I don't recall that many words were exchanged between us, and then I was asked to begin. As the brief piano introduction to *Non so piu cosa son* (an aria from *Le Nozze di Figaro* by Mozart) sounded, I took a deep breath and opened my mouth, expecting to hear my first notes sailing out into the darkness. Instead, nothing happened. There was no sound. What a surprise and shock. I was asked to begin again. And again, the same thing happened. Confused and embarrassed, I tried one more time to sing. But my voice failed me. This had never happened to me before, so I was absolutely dumbfounded and mortified. I sensed the discomfort reflected back to me by my jurors. Afraid that I would burst into tears, and not knowing what else to do, I quickly walked off the stage. No words of support or understanding or explanation were offered to me by my judge and jury. I just knew that I had failed this most important exam and didn't have a clue about what was happening to me.

Though the Conservatory Dean urged me to stay, I decided to transfer to the large state university where my high school boyfriend was a student. Fleeing to safety was a knee-jerk reaction. The music department there paled in comparison to the high standards of the Conservatory, but I needed to get out of the city and away from a musical environment that felt judgmental and competitive and in which I had lost any paltry amount of confidence I might have had. So, I settled for less, worked through most of the requirements for a degree in music education, became pregnant at

19, and married my high school boyfriend, who was as unready for marriage and parenting as I was. After carrying my baby girl around in a pouch and breast-feeding her in the back of darkened lecture halls, I eventually dropped out of my final year of undergraduate university to stay home and be a wife and mother. But before that happened, I had again 'lost my voice' while singing in the University Chorale during my pregnancy.

It would take me many years to unravel the causes of my voice loss as a young woman. While living through it, I couldn't make sense of it. Moving from one seeming disaster to the next, I was just too busy trying to keep it all together to be able to recognize the deep state of stress and anxiety I was in. I soon left my ill-fated marriage, found a job as a secretary at a nearby college, put my daughter in day care, and was miserable and lonely. Music was the furthest thing from my mind. I didn't even have a piano. I had arrived at a place in my life where I had no support, no meaningful work, not enough emotional health and maturity to be a strong parent, and no music. No wonder I was so sad.

TWO

INFORMATIVE STRUGGLES

THE DECADE THROUGH MY TWENTIES was full of episodes of adventure and learning, heartbreak and poverty. Yearning to find some solid ground, I struck out in one direction followed by another. Always looking for love, my personal life was chaotic and difficult. My little daughter and I lived communally for several years while I finished my undergraduate degree in music. The silver lining of transferring to the university was my introduction to an interest in psychology and personal inner work. My early studies in group counseling and feminism opened a door to the work I needed to do on myself in order to find a truer and healthier way in my life. The social changes of the 1970s swept me along as I dabbled in disappointing relationships with totally inappropriate men, played piano in rock 'n' roll bands (with one of my brothers), and basically stumbled through my young adulthood, with daughter in tow. I still hadn't a clue how music was going to play out in my life, given the accidental way I found myself playing loud music in cheap bars, bored by the basic chordal structures of the music of the times. I tried using my voice in this setting but knew that forcing my vocal chords was probably the worst thing I could have been doing with my fragile instrument. It was a wild time, an important growing time in my life, but very difficult indeed.

It wasn't until I moved myself and my daughter to the Pacific Northwest, Oregon, that everything started to change in my musical life for the better. Bruce Kramer, a very wise musician and man who recently died of ALS, wrote, "Struggles are informative. They determine the pathways that will be taken."[1]

Struggles are informative.
They determine the pathways that will be taken.

— Bruce Kramer

I now see these early years of my life as a period of struggle that primed me for what was to follow—the discovery of a new musical path that would eventually lead to my true calling as a Musician Healer. A shamanic path is always founded on a period of suffering and challenge, be it serious illness, physical or psychological, or deep experiences of loss or terror. We learn neither compassion, nor the ability to use deep powers within us, without first walking through hot fires and surviving. And that's what I was doing.

Taking a grand leap from East coast to West, without anything in the way of financial resources, was the risky shake-up that was needed to set me in a new and

[1] Bruce Kramer. *We Know How This Ends: Living While Dying.* University of Minnesota Press. 2015.

better direction. Nearing thirty years old, I decided to finally get back to some serious music study, and to focus on the piano while my voice remained dormant, in a state of bewildered rest. After settling in Eugene, Oregon in the mid-seventies, I met a young man who was doing a spiritual practice in Buddhist teachings. He played the sitar and told me about a very special Elder woman who taught piano to all the more advanced pianists in town, among them the piano faculty at the University of Oregon. As fortune would have it, she took me under her wing. Her name was Pauline Dahl Norris, and hers is a fascinating and inspirational story.

Pauline Dahl Norris

Pauline Dahl was born in a small village in northern British Columbia on April 27, 1892. Her mother, Ethel Gertrude Dahl, was an accomplished violinist and teacher who had followed her husband from the USA to Canada to mine for silver. Ethel was the only music teacher for many miles around and taught whatever instrument was brought to her: violin, banjo, guitar, as well as voice and piano. Pauline told me, "My mother was a genius and child prodigy, while growing up in Wisconsin. By age 12, she was touring and teaching 40-year-old men the subtleties of inspired musicianship and expression."

Marrying and following her husband into the wilds of Canada had brought great strain into Ethel's life. As Pauline put it, her father was "always hunting down one mine or another." The little family always ended up in tiny villages, where, as she said, "there were no pianos, only Indians." They eventually settled in Rossland BC, a silver-mining town just across the border from Washington state. During these years of Pauline's childhood, her mother suffered from bouts of nervous exhaustion. I can well imagine how such a gifted woman must have felt stifled and unsupported in her art, given her husband's lifestyle and the mores of the time. Psychiatric breakdowns would pepper Ethel's life for many years, witnessed by an adoring daughter who learned much from her mother, her first music teacher.

Pauline remembered standing outside the closed door to the parlor, listening to all the music lessons her mother taught. As a younger child, her mother did not realize how interested Pauline was in music. But Pauline showed up for every lesson her mother taught—sometimes forty a week—and initially learned through a closed door. When Ethel finally became aware of Pauline's interest and passion, she began giving her proper lessons at a piano, which was brought to them, piece by piece, from some far-off place in the province. She also taught her violin and voice, revealing a sweet high soprano. But it was the piano that the child Pauline truly loved and wished to master.

By 1905, the family had relocated to Chicago, where Pauline could study with 'the greats.' Ethel was determined to nourish her daughter's musical talent to the fullest. Still very young, only 13 years old, Pauline began piano study with Rudolph Ganz, famed conductor, pianist, and composer. Her mother, in the meantime, established herself as a much-in-demand music teacher in the city. My sense is that her father may have continued his wandering ways at this time, enabling the two women to carry on their musical quest without disruption. But again, Ethel experienced a terrible nervous breakdown and was unable to continue her teaching. Still a teenager, Pauline took on all her mothers' students to save the day. It was in this way that she herself became a teacher. I find it interesting that Pauline and I were the resilient ones in our troubled childhood families, picking up the pieces during our mothers' bouts with depression.

Despite her more practical duties as piano teacher, a concert career was still within the realm of possibility for young Pauline, she was that gifted. Rudolph Ganz set up an audition for her to play for the great master Federico Busoni, in hopes of passing Pauline on as his student. The strong musical background bestowed by her mother was a powerful foundation upon which to build. And she was becoming a rising star, a prodigy who was already presenting notable concerts in the city. On the evening before her scheduled audition with Busoni, she and her mother took a walk along the railroad tracks to relax and clear their minds of music. They stopped to rest, and as they were talking, Pauline lay her hand on the rail. Suddenly the rails shifted, and her fourth finger on the left hand was severed at the tip. To her great disappointment, she missed her audition with Maestro Busoni. It was not to be. But in her persevering way, despite warnings from her doctors that her finger might never heal properly, she continued practicing and strengthening the digit, until she was nearly whole again. To everyone's amazement, six months after her fateful accident, Pauline played with the Chicago Symphony Orchestra. What courage and strength this young woman had. Perhaps this was Pauline's shamanic episode of trauma, one of the great challenges she had to face and surmount in order to realize her highest powers.

I know only about her earlier years, since she told me little about her adult life, other than that she had been married three times, twice to the same man. Her first husband simply left without a trace and being a woman of post-Victorian times and strongly influenced by a mother who wanted to see her daughter taken care of, she married again, divorced, then remarried the same man. She told me that neither of her husbands truly understood her or her musical passion. But there was another man, in the background, Clarence, who was very special to her. He supported her work and art in every way he could, and I believe he must have been her true love. Pauline had only one child, a daughter named Frances. Just like me: one girl-child from a line of mostly disappointing relationships with men. She once told me,

> As women, we'd like to believe that we can share our every thought and dream with the man we love. But this is not wise, for it's impossible for there to be total understanding between a man and woman. They are opposites. It is wiser for a woman to be silent, to hold fast to her dream and work towards its realization unceasingly, but with discretion.

The long story of how women have had to fight for their rightful place in this world, for the full satisfaction of being all that we can be, is reflected in Pauline's life. And in mine.

Wasn't it my great good fortune to cross this wonderful woman's path so many, many years later, after she had experienced the fullness of life and work? She was 86 years old, arthritic in the hands and crippled in one foot when I studied with her but she had so much love and wisdom to share. The most remarkable thing I remember about Pauline Dahl Norris is the way her body was transformed from old and disabled, to light and free whenever she played. Somehow her stiff and painful fingers forgot their age when she played the *Aeolian Étude* of Chopin. She was indeed transported to another state of being at the keyboard, one that transcended the limitations of an aged body. Her spirit was visibly lit, and the music she made was beyond beautiful. I wanted so much to be like that. Perhaps the most important teaching she gave me was this:

> Dream of yourself perfectly free of obstruction in your body, especially in the chest and shoulders. Place yourself in that dream body, use your powerful imagination, and then play.

Three Origins

It was during this time that I co-created an art piece called "Three Origins" with a dancer friend of mine, Ena Sherlin, a collaborative work that incorporated original poetry, music, and dance. We were both heading toward our 30th birthdays and wanted to mark the time by creating and performing an initiation piece at the local Unitarian Church, where I often played on

Sundays. Ena and I liked writing short poems, were interested in things spiritual and psychic, and were artists, so our friendship was fast. Like Pauline, Ena had suffered an accident on a subway rail some years before, which severed part of her foot, an interesting synchronicity. As a Denishawn dancer—another uncanny synchronicity since I too had studied Denishawn dance, a fairly obscure offshoot of ballet, as a child—Ena had to strengthen her foot and learn to dance again with a disability. Many parallels were obvious in these relationships I was cultivating.

Ena and I meditated, at a distance from each other, while we were composing this work and used psychic practices to conjure meaning to what we were creating together. From the work's inception, the number 3 was a clear and guiding force. Numerologically, it is the symbol for spirit, and the influence of otherworldly dimensions on this creative process was strongly felt by both of us. While we opened ourselves to being channels for some Greater Voice, we were given experiential glimpses of a more highly evolved state of human being.

One of the cryptic messages we received was, "see empty people/ hear even people/seek mystery body." It appeared that we were being initiated into a new level of knowledge that called for a lifetime of pondering and experiencing, to more fully understand. What was clear, even during our earliest encounters with the Mystery Body, was that it embodied a trinity of forces body, mind, and spirit. Each was distinct from, yet interrelated with the others. When these forces operated free of debris, obstruction and tension, and maintained a flexible flow of energetic equilibrium, the Mystery Body emerged. The sum was much larger than its parts; this new human entity surpassed anything our species had evolutionarily achieved to date.[2]

It's now obvious, all these years later, that the seeds of understanding that were planted within my conscious and unconscious self by Pauline Dahl Norris were showing up in the "Three Origins" artistic collaboration with Ena. Clearing away obstruction within all levels of our being was the way to proceed. In this way, Pauline passed a very bright torch to me, one that I've carried now for many years. My dear teacher and friend finally died at the advanced age of 102, and although I had lost touch with her some years before that event, her spirit and wisdom has accompanied me throughout my journey of discovery and realization. Forever indebted am I.

Learning to Teach

While still in Oregon, I began to take on private piano students and offered piano accompaniment for singers and instrumentalists. A generous friend offered financial help so I could buy a secondhand grand piano. I was feeling my way through all this change, getting to know the needs of the various people who came to me for instruction and support—and I was learning how to teach. It became clear very early on, whether I was teaching young ones or adults, that I was as interested in helping others to free themselves of troublesome attitudes, emotions, and physical obstructions while at the keyboard (and perhaps in other parts of their lives) as I was in sharing my knowledge of music and play-

[2] Islene Runningdeer. "Music as Medicine: Learning the Songs of the Self." Master's Thesis, University of Vermont, pp. 34-35.

ing an instrument. The youngsters were afraid of making mistakes and the adults carried within themselves a self-conscious fear stemming from recollections of unhappy experiences taking music lessons as children. I thought, *Why is there so much trauma attached to this beautiful creative act? What can I do to help these folks put down all the stress so they can begin to enjoy the process of making music?*

Thus began many years of teaching, all the while incorporating relaxation, imagery, and deep breathing techniques at the keyboard. While teaching others, I deepened my own such practice, and we became better, freer musicians together. I always encouraged my students to learn music that they loved, while introducing them to the music I loved. There's no sense spending all that time and energy on something that doesn't inspire and fill us. Each person's musical tastes are different, and that needs to be honored, and used for further growth. We practiced laughing when we played wrong notes. And over time, the laughter was no longer necessary, and we learned to simply shrug the blunder away and carry on.

One of my young, 9-year-old students, Christine, made me a funny, wonderful card, using one of my quotes: "Life is full of missed notes!", which I've saved all these years. My students helped me to understand that accepting our failings with levity and a smile enables us to take greater risks, to try new things, to put everything in a more balanced perspective. We do not have to prove perfection. In fact, we can never reach perfection on this plane. We can just do our best, and then, our better.

As I worked in a therapeutic way with my students, it became obvious that this different way of being at the piano was taking hold in other places in their daily lives. People were speaking up for themselves more, one man, a singer, lost 100 lbs. of unhealthy weight during just one year of working with me. Some became happier and more confident. My young-girl students were less afraid of playing for others and really proud of what they were accomplishing. The fear of judgment was something I had worked very hard to eliminate in my studio, and it truly paid off in big dividends. When it was time for me to move back to my home in New England, I regretted leaving behind Pauline and my wonderful little entourage of students. They had all taught me so very much about how I could use my musical talents to help others. Again, forever indebted.

While I continued teaching, I worked several church posts, providing keyboard music for worship. I was raised in a French-Canadian Catholic family but had moved away from organized religion while still in my teens. I was much more interested in finding my own spiritual path, and forever a rebel at heart, I thought I might be able to add something new and fresh to the traditional religious environments where I was employed. I began playing from the classical piano repertoire, offering Chopin preludes, Brahms intermezzi, Mozart sonata movements, and the like, during the meditative prelude section of each service. I was surprised by the response, which was not at all resistant. In fact, worshippers approached me after service and thanked me for such beautiful music. Some of them cried with gratitude, clasped my hands, and hugged me warmly. So I carried on in this way, and played all sorts of fine pieces, from Scarlatti and Ravel, to Debussy, sometimes even Bix Beiderbecke piano jazz from the 1930s and '40s. I began to see that my music, played from a more open and freer place within myself, had powerful effects on my listeners. Not only did the congregation provide me with a weekly opportunity to share a kind of musical healing with my audience, it also gave me a way to practice 'giving away' my music, making it a gift to others. This was not a performance, as such. It grew to be something deeper and better, I think. My years playing in churches showed me that I could do things my own way, as long as I respected the integrity of a particular form of worship, while at the same time revealing to others that spiritual beauty comes in many guises.

Mysteries of Life and Death

While the healing effects of my music were becoming more obvious, an adult piano student of mine, Mark, told me of a hospice volunteer training he was about to sign up for. I asked more questions and decided to join him. My spiritual road had led me to wonder about the deep mysteries of life and death. I was easily drawn to learning more about death and dying and the special care that hospice provides. Mark was a personal link to this new fork in the road. (Forever indebted, again.)

I found that I felt very much at home in the presence of those who were dying and the families who were caring for them. With my hospice volunteer certificate in hand, I began working with my first patient, who just so happened to have an old upright piano at his bedside. Carl was bedridden, with brain cancer, and loved music. So I played for him.

I quickly realized that this was work I wanted to continue doing and developing. But I also realized that, unless I had an advanced degree in something related to healing, I'd have a difficult time finding work in medicine, particularly palliative and hospice care. In my mid-forties I entered graduate school, beefed up some skills in counseling and writing, developmental psychology and stress management, and did my thesis research on music and medicine. With degree in hand, and much better prepared, I managed to generate some work for myself on the Central Vermont Hospice and Palliative Care Team. That was the beginning of many years of applying music as medicine for people at the end of life. In another book I wrote titled *Musical Encounters with Dying: Stories and Lessons* (Jessica Kingsley Publishers, 2013) I chronicle numerous experiences with the dying and their families. I won't go into great detail here, but what is important to say is that healing on many levels occurs when music is applied with a deep intention to calm and comfort those who are suffering. Fear and anxiety can be softened, tears and laughter can be released, bodily pains can be temporarily forgotten, breathing difficulty can be eased, memories of a long life can be evoked, connection among family members can be supported, and even spiritual transformation can occur.

The end of life is a very interesting and important part of life. It can be very full and rich, but it can also be lonely and discouraging. I love working with people and music, shining a light on emotions, memory, relaxation, and spiritual exploration and preparation; all this comes into play when I work with those at the end of life. This is healing, in the most comprehensive sense. This is the work that finally, over many years of practice, led me to the realization that I am, after all, a Musician Healer.

Becoming a Musician Healer

I am not naive, nor presumptuous. I know that presenting myself as a Musician Healer to the conventional medical world will most likely raise more than a few eyebrows. So, I identify myself, in most professional settings, as a therapeutic musician or music therapist. Sometimes this can get a little confusing, since my way of finding myself into this kind of work was not through the more conventional academic avenues for that role.

What I do is, in many ways, similar to what a Certified Music Therapist, with a degree in such, does. But some things we do are different from one another. I have wisely taken from standard music therapy the principles and practices that relate to the area of medicine I work in, which is palliative and Elder care, and which also enrich my style of working with people. What else I've added to my education and preparation is of my own design.

I was really fortunate to be able to obtain a Master of Education degree through the Interdisciplinary Program at the Graduate School of the University of Vermont. I took courses from the medical, counseling/psychology, and education schools there, as I was already quite well-prepared in music as a classically trained pianist and singer. In-depth spiritual study and practice over many years, in Native American spirituality, Buddhism, Taoism, Hinduism, Gnostic Christianity, as well as my childhood education as a Catholic and Christian, have helped me to feel more connected to an inner world of deep consciousness, gratitude, and awe. This eclectic mix of spiritual orientation helps me to relate to many different kinds of people, with or without belief.

I am proud of the way I've followed my own road in this big endeavor; that I've had the good sense to blend conventional academic and medical worlds with the more esoteric traditions that I cherish. When I feel free of the strictures of the more conventional world, I much more honestly call myself a Musician Healer, because that's what I truly am. So let's take a closer look at who and what a Musician Healer is. Where she came from, how she works, and what she aspires to.

THREE

ANCIENT EGYPT

WHATEVER HAPPENED to all the ancient healing wisdom of times and cultures past? It strikes me as strange and wasteful that with the advent of modern Western medicine, a mere century or so ago, so much of value was tossed aside. It was apparently quite easy, in the name of progress and allopathy, to throw many babies out with the bath water. Deemed witchery or superstition, proponents of modern medicine have done a good job of disenfranchising any other healing paradigm based on ancient belief and practice.

Midwifery, for example, perhaps the most ancient healing practice of all, virtually disappeared from modern medicine for decades in the twentieth century. And as a result, I, and many other women, experienced an unsupported, disconnected, and powerless birthing in a hospital. My grandmother birthed my mother in her own bed, with the competent coaching and expertise of another woman to give her confidence. But beyond the 1920s, and as late as the late 1960s, birthing in the most economically advanced countries was relocated to hospitals where doctors could more easily deal with complications, but also where the natural act of bringing a baby into the world became a much less humane process involving drugs, forceps, and isolation. It was as if the doctor became the one to birth the child, not the mother. My awful ordeal of being left alone in a sterile labor room for many hours, flat on my back and pumped with Demerol, staring up at a big black institutional wall clock, is a terrible memory forever etched in my mind, colored by the emotions of fear and helplessness. Fortunately, soon after I birthed my only child, midwifery was re-embraced as a worthwhile and legitimate (ancient) medical practice, but not without a lot of clamoring insistence from the women of my generation and those who followed me.

Much the same sort of dismissal happened with music as a healing practice. But unlike midwifery, which needs no further explanation or defense within today's medical institutions, I still find myself educating, demonstrating, and validating my healing practice, most especially with medical colleagues, some of whom continue to think of what I do as entertainment, and not medicine. Stereotypical images of superstition and primitive ritual, coupled with a derisive attitude, have been very effectively implanted in the mainstream mind by our modern allopathic culture, which to this day still claims medicine as its exclusive domain—much like fundamental religions in the twenty-first century. This has made it more than difficult to reintroduce some of the ancient holistic therapies, adapted for today's world, into our conventional medical facilities.

Granted, change is happening. I wouldn't be doing what I do in a hospital setting if there weren't open minded, interested doctors and administrators out there who appreciate the ways in which allopathic medicine and updated ancient healing practices (which they call complementary medicine) can work together. Still, too many medical professionals still don't know, understand, or appreciate what bringing a new version of ancient medical wisdom into the mix could do to make the work of modern healing more powerful and effective.

To illustrate this divide, several years ago I attended a public forum on medicine led by then Surgeon General Dr. Everett Koop. After he spoke about new advances in medicine to a small crowd of about one hundred, outside the august library of a prestigious New England Ivy League college, he opened the floor to questions. I'd waved my hand for a long time when he finally called on me. I asked,

> Dr. Koop, I'm wondering if you think that complementary modalities such as music therapy, and others, will be included any time soon in the array of services available to patients in various hospital settings?

He said, without much consideration, "Well, there's a lot of voodoo out there that I wouldn't want in my hospital." Plenty of laughter gave way to his finally saying, "Well, of course, I don't mean to say that music is voodoo, but...." Besides being made the butt of his joke and feeling a rush of insult and anger, I realized that I had just been given a perfect example of how a very influential allopathic doctor held an attitude of disdain for complementary medicine, and any modality that hearkened back to ancient times, and couldn't even talk about it seriously. This was quite a few years ago, granted, but there is still resistance out there, and I'd love to see it disappear, for all our sakes.

***

THE ANCIENTS, AND PEOPLE of Indigenous cultures, have much wise light to shed on how we ought to be going about healing the sick, restoring the depressed and fearful, preparing one another for death and whatever is to follow. It's high time we open our minds and hearts to this knowledge, and then refashion it to serve our modern purposes. This is what I have done in creating my own healing work with music and sound, drawing from the ways of the long ago past, while practicing my own version in the world of now.

In the spirit of elevating the positions of ancient healers—and us modern healers who descend from them—let's go back in time and take a look at four different healing practices and practitioners. Over the next chapters, unique cultural settings and personalities within these eras will be observed in terms of how they used music and sound, meshed with a heavy dose of spiritual belief, to bring aid to the suffering.

Retracing our steps, before moving forward, is often well indicated. I recently unearthed a paper I'd written twenty years ago, while in graduate school, about the contents of the Greek Magical Papyri. In these ancient texts are found magical incantations to be offered vocally for purposes of healing the sick and supporting the dying. These are songs and recitations which aim to cast out daimons of disease, while imploring the gods to provide aid and strength. The will and prayer of the healer is carried on the waves of song; the vocal sounds that are delivered from the healer's body are fueled by the breath (spirit). Many call this magic, others superstition. But it was medicine of a high order many centuries ago.

Ancient practitioners addressed
not only physical ailments but the emotional
and spiritual components that were related.

The ancient Egyptians and Greeks traded secrets, syncretizing their cultures as they developed healing practices. Many incantations focusing on vocalizing vowel sounds, *"AAA EEE III OOO UUU,"* can be found in the Egyptian and Greek Medical Papyri, which have been discovered in more modern times. These open sounds carry the exhaled breath of the musician/singer in a potent way. Also included in these papyri are verses and hymns which were either spoken or sung, to implore the goddesses and gods to aid in whatever intention was cited, be it of a medical nature or otherwise. Some incantations had to do with attracting love, keeping bugs out of the house, subduing anger, asking for a dream oracle, for good outcomes, and the like.

Because herbal and other natural remedies, primitive surgery, spiritual belief and magic were combined to effect the most successful healing, ancient practitioners addressed not only physical ailments but the emotional and spiritual components that were related. The Divine was never far from any activity. Sounding the magical vowels on a vocal tone directed the breath, and powerful intention of the healer, into the patient, delivering spiritual energy in the process. We inspire and expire; we breathe in spirit and breathe out spirit. Our spirits enter our bodies at birth with the first inhalation. And leave our bodies at death with the final exhalation. It is no wonder, then, that the human voice, supported by the breath, has been an instrument of healing throughout the ages and was of particular import in the four-thousand-year-long civilization of ancient Egypt.

While looking back, I rediscovered an old book, titled *Initiation*, by Elisabeth Haich. It has been sitting on my bookshelf, untouched, for more than forty years now. But its initial impact never left me. Haich was a beloved teacher of the esoteric. In this book, written in the 1960s, she explored her past life memory of being a musician/priestess/healer in ancient Egypt, and how it impacted her modern-day life. Fact or fiction, who is to say? Her story is rich in detail, her characters are recalled as vividly as one might remember close friends or relatives who have passed on to another realm. It tells the tale of her initiation as a young woman into the mysteries of sacred healing, using sound and music.

When I initially read this book, at the beginning of my own quest regarding such things, I was completely taken in by the possibility that Haich had indeed experienced this lifetime ages ago, only to find herself again in this more-modern lifetime, continuing to teach and practice her own brand of healing and empowerment. So many years later, it is indeed strange and wonderful that her book opened its pages to me again, after four decades of developing my own brand of healing with sound and music—as if there is something more here to understand, to share.

Egyptian *Shemayet*

It's time to bring *Shemayet* to center stage, the title given to women musician/priestess/healers from ancient Egypt. In many ways, *Shemayet* is a prototype for what I do in my healing work today, thousands of years after *Shemayet* walked the earth. Who might she be?

I will call her Nenet, a 17-year-old woman, named for the goddess of the deep. She lived in Dendera, in the southern Nile valley near the great center of Thebes, with her father, grandmother, and younger sister. The time was around 2000 BCE.

Nenet was born from a long line of Shemayet and Priestesses. Her mother, Pu-ra, died from complications of childbirth when Nenet was 10 years old. Pu-ra was a beautiful singer who had served as temple musician (*Shemayet*) at the nearby Temple of Hathor. Unfortunate and ironic was this young mother's death, despite the high incidence of childbirth mortality in ancient Egypt. Hathor was the goddess of fertility, childbirth, and motherhood, and Pu-ra had offered her voice and harp for the pleasure and appeasement of Hathor for ten years of her short life, beseeching the goddess to protect all women and children at this dangerous time.

Nenet's father, Hetep, was a well-respected *swnw*,

or physician. He specialized in gynecology, pediatrics, and diseases of the eye. He grieved the loss of his wife. Although he had cared for her health conscientiously during her pregnancy, she died from excessive bleeding after a long and hard labor. Men were not allowed to be present during childbirth, not even *swnw*, and he remembered well having to shut the door and allow the Elder women to minister to his beloved wife as she gave birth and then died.

Nenet's grandmother, Ama, was one of these Elder women. She had been a Priestess and *Shemayet* in the sacred Temple while she was young, but failing eyesight kept her closer to home in her later years. Still, she continued to serve her family and community by attending local births with other Elder women who assisted the natural process of bringing life into the world. They had done all they could for her daughter, Pu-ra, but on that night, Hathor and Bes and Heqet (all goddesses of childbirth) were disagreeable and deaf to their incantations and prayers. Ama devoted the rest of her days to her surviving family, and most especially to Nenet and her little sister.

This was a family of high regard in Dendera. Although some *swnw* and *Shemayet* provided service exclusively to the royal families, Nenet's family served the common populace. They were well-educated, literate, and skilled public servants who were dedicated to supporting the health and wellbeing of their community with the help of their gods. In return, they received an ample share of goods and services, lived in a comfortable house, and enjoyed a respected position in their society.

Although still a young woman, Nenet's responsibilities were many. She shared the care of her younger sister with her Ama (grandmother) as well as the cooking and other household duties. But this was only a portion of her daily life. Her mother had taught her to sing the sacred hymns to Hathor and to recite the many incantations that were used in her father's medical practice to heal the sick. While still alive, Pu-ra regularly accompanied her husband to the homes of his patients, providing sacred sound and music to fortify the spirits of the sick while their bodies were strengthened by the herbal remedies administered by Hetep.

From the time of her mother's death, young Nenet developed her own practice by offering song, harp, and sistrum (a percussive rattling instrument) at the Temple of Hathor, along with other young *Shemayet* in training. Her best friend was among this group, and practicing the hymns and incantations together was, at first, merely play for them, but grew eventually to be very serious business.

The Sacred and Divine

Divinity was never far from any activity in ancient Egypt so blended were the world of the gods and goddesses and the everyday lives of men and women. Medicine embraced the sacred presence incorporated in the powerful, soothing sounds of music, perhaps wisely so, since herbal remedies and very basic surgery alone had limited or no effect when it came to treating the serious diseases of the day. These early people seemed to have understood and

The Caduceus was adopted by many cultural healing practices throughout the ages.

depended upon the ability of the mind to help heal the body. Something that we are finally remembering and retrieving today.

On her 13th birthday, Hetep began taking Nenet on visits to his patients. He missed the holy musical ministrations of his wife and knew he could depend upon his young daughter to fill her space. He also gifted her with Pu-ra's golden amulet, the caduceus, which she wore on her left arm. This ancient Egyptian symbol of two snakes, representing male and female energy spiraling around a golden central rod, was adopted by many cultural healing practices throughout the ages. Practitioners of kundalini yoga, for example, understand it to mean the rising of vital energy through the body chakras into the spiritual realm of enlightenment. Although not quite seen in the same light, the American Medical Society uses it today as its organization's symbol and a variation of this symbol, with one snake coiled around a staff, is used as a Cap badge of the British Royal Army Medical Corps.

Nenet was a willing and eager participant in this serious work and paid close attention to learning something about her father's skill as well as perfecting her musical medicine. She liked to study the contents of Hetep's medical library at home, which included many old papyri scribed by *swnw* who had preceded him, some going back even a thousand years. Medical practice had remained pretty much the same all that time, but whenever Hetep experimented with something new, he would record his own findings, to be passed along to practitioners who would follow him. In this way, three thousand years of practical and sacred medicine was recorded, copies of which were buried in the tombs of *swnw*. In the early years of the twentieth century, archaeologists began discovering these ancient records in tombs that were opened in the Nile Valley. How fortunate for us to now have access to this esoteric treasure. I can read translations today of ancient papyri that Nenet may have studied under lamplight four thousand years ago.

Nenet certainly missed her mother and had a special bond with Ama. Knowing so well the dangers of childbirth and how it often took the lives of dear ones, she naturally explored her interest in the midwifery of the day. Her grandmother was honored to teach her this special craft and was most eager to be able to add Nenet's sacred music and incantation to her birthing visits. Sometimes these visits came in the middle of the night, and Nenet was a trustworthy companion for Ama, in her blindness, while making their way through the streets of Dendera. While father remained sleeping at home with her young sister, these two women, young and old, helped many mothers and newborns to enact a safe birth. After cleaning the child, and tending to delivering the placenta from the mother, her father would be summoned to take over their continuing health care. Nenet and Ama were then free to return home to their beds for sleep. This family was a fine team, loved and depended upon by many. They contributed much to the safety and health of their neighbors and larger community, while enjoying the satisfaction of working together as a close-knit group. They all agreed that this work was not only in honor of the gods but in remembrance of Pu-ra, who had done the same.

Nenet's Songs

Before I leave Nenet to the foggy mist of ancient history, here are translations of a hymn and incantations that she may have voiced in her work. They were found in various medical papyri or inscribed on stone tablets in hieroglyph. Imagine a young woman, breathing deeply as she intones these sounds, shaking a sistrum with a steady soothing beat, and swaying with the energy she is directing to one who is resting in bed. While, in my practice today, I do not seek to cast out the same daimons of Nenet's imagination, lesser supernatural beings, minor gods, or spirits of dead heroes, I do acknowledge that stress, trauma, viruses and bacteria, environmental toxins, heredity can also be thought of as daimons. These dangerous factors can lead to much illness in the world, and my modern-day medicine seeks to neutralize and cast out these malevolent forces, while relieving their symptomatic effects. I also summon the aid of my own spiritual helpers, as I envision them, and add that to my strong will and intent as I minister to the sick. And like Nenet, I work alongside the doctors who administer their medicines, all with strong hopes and intentions.

I can easily see myself in her. So, let's bow to her wisdom, and "listen" to her chant these incantations:

FOR ASCENT OF THE UTERUS

> I conjure you, O Womb, by the one established over the Abyss, before heaven, earth, sea, light, or darkness came to be; you who created the angels, being foremost *AMICHAMCHOU* and *CHOUCHAO CHEROEI OUEICHO ODOU PROSEIOGGES,* and who sit over the cherubim, who bear your own throne, that you return again to your seat, and that you do not turn, to one side, into the right part of the ribs, or into the left part of the ribs, and that you do not gnaw into the heart like a dog, but remain indeed in your own intended and proper place.... I conjure by the one who, in the beginning, made the heaven and earth and all that is therein. Hallelujah! Amen!

Nenet might have sung, recited, or written these incantations on a tin tablet while working at the bedside of a woman giving birth.

HYMN TO THE SEVEN HATHORS
(goddesses of fertility, childbirth)

We beat the framedrum
for Her spirit
we dance
for Her majesty
we raise high Her image
to the heights of heaven
it is She who is
the Lady of the Sekhem sistra
and the menat
the Lady of the Naos sistrum
music is made for Her ka (life energy)
we worship Her majesty
making offerings from sunset to dawn
it is She who is
the lady of joyful music
the lady of the iab-dance
the lady of sounding the sistrum
the lady of singers
the lady of the kheb-dance
the lady of weaving garlands
the lady of beauty
the lady of the keskes dance
when Her two eyes open :
the sun and the moon
our hearts rejoice in seeing the light
it is She who is the lady of the dance wreaths
the lady of those who are drunk with joy
we do not dance and drum for any other
we devote ourselves to Her divine spirit alone

Nenet may have sung this hymn, with sister *Shemayet,* in the Temple of Hathor in Dendera. A special chamber in the temple, a birth house called the mammisi, was reserved for pregnant women who wished to pray to Hathor for a successful and healthy birth. Nenet may have sung within these walls many times.

FOUR

HAUDENOSAUNEE

ONATAH, Corn Spirit Daughter, was an Atetshent, a Dreamer. She possessed great Orenda, or magical healing power. She was a member of the Seneca tribe, one of the Five Nations that comprised the Iroquois/Haudenosaunee Confederacy. She lived in a longhouse with nine other families of the Bear clan. The year was 1499 AD.

Donehogawa, He Who Guards the Gate of Sunset, lived in the same longhouse with his family. His mother was sister to Onatah. He too was an Atetshent, a Dreamer, and an honored member of The Little Water Medicine Society, where he had a special role as keeper of the Sacred Medicine Bundle.

The people in this matrilineal society believed in the ultimate power of the Dream. Before anything appeared in creation, it was dreamed. Before anyone was healed of sickness, it was dreamed. Before a major decision about the community was made, it was dreamed. Onatah and Donehogawa looked for guidance and direction in their dreams and shared what they experienced during sleep with the community at large, as did everyone else, after waking. They literally lived in two worlds: the world of the Earth and the world of spiritual power. When both worlds were in balance, all was well. The soul's longing for well-being, *On-no-kwat,* was the true meaning of medicine. And when the soul is in balance with all of Creation, physical health and well-being is maintained.

Atetshent was a special kind of Dreamer. He or she was also a doctor, a sorcerer, or a shaman—one whose job it was to fulfill her patient's soul's desire for wellness. Healing was done with plant remedies, sacred ceremony, song, rattles and drums, dancing, and a powerful appeal to the supernatural world of spirit.

To boost the powers of the precious plants,
she sang the healing songs handed down to her
through many generations as well as the new songs
gifted to her in her own dreams.

A healer was assisted by Oki, special animal spirits who injected Orenda, or spiritual power, into the process of doctoring. The songs used in healing ceremonies were received in Dreams, and taught from mother to daughter, father to son, down the long line of descendants. It is not known just how old these ceremonies and songs are, but it is most certainly true that they are ancient. Indications for herbal remedies were also given in Dreams, as were the expected outcomes of treatment. Both recovery and death were seen in Dreams. The Haudenosaunee people lived with a very different mind, heart, and spirit set than we do in the modern technological world. To them, the Dreamworld was as real, perhaps even more real, than the Wakingworld. Each balanced the other, generating more and more *Maskan*, or the ability to do extraordinary things, into the People.

Onatah and Donehogawa used their Dreams to increase their *Maskan*. Onatah was especially successful with plant cures, as were many Bear clan members, having learned where to pick and how to apply special herbs from her mother and grandmother. She assisted the sick, the dying, the wounded, and women in childbirth, using her plant knowledge and directing powerful energy into those suffering. To boost the powers of the precious plants, she sang the healing songs handed down to her through many generations as well as the new songs gifted to her in her own dreams.

Donehogawa and twelve other men who were members of the Little Water Medicine Society were called upon by Onatah and other women of authority (the *gantowisas*) when a special healing was necessary. At their behest, The Medicine Society conducted all-day-and-night-long ceremonies, with song, rattles (recall the sistrum of the ancient Egyptians), and dance which boosted the efforts of the other tribal healers. The Sacred Medicine Bundle, which contained ancient natural artifacts and a special medicine made of a secret herbal compound, was central to the ceremony. It held the accumulated power of unnumbered generational keeping. After each healing it had attended throughout the generations, it was rejuvenated and strengthened with more singing and ritual. In this way, its efficacy and power were faithfully maintained by the tribe. The Medicine Bundle that Donehogawa kept secure had been handed down by a long line of his ancestors and was considered a most precious and sacred treasure.

Onatah and Kajijonhawe Dream

On this night in 1499 AD (I wonder how the people marked the number of that year?), Onatah was kneeling at the bedrobes of her grandmother, Kajijonhawe, Bouquet Carrier, an Elder Gantowisa who was stricken with a disease of the lung. Onatah had been singing through the night. The winter had been especially harsh, cold, and long, and food supplies were dwindling. Grandmother had contracted pneumonia; all the known herbal remedies that helped with difficult breathing had been administered, but her strength was waning and Onatah saw the clear signs of approaching death. She had seen her grandmother's death in last night's dream also, and sensed that it was the sign she needed to ask for Donehogawa's help.

Kajijonhawe herself had dreamed of walking down a new road, accompanied by her animal spirit, and was preparing to leave her earthly body with anticipation and acceptance. She woke briefly in the night, spoke of her dream, and she and Otanah agreed that a healing ceremony should be conducted by the Little Water Society singers and dancers. The longing of her soul was for a safe transition back to the Sky and Stars, and those keepers of the Sacred Medicine Bundle could help her achieve this.

Long before first dawn's light, Donehogawa summoned the other men of the society, visiting each longhouse where they dwelled. The Sacred Medicine Bundle, turtle shell rattles and drums, were brought to Kajijonhawe's longhouse, where members of her clan lined up on both sides of the structure to witness the ritual. Donehogawa offered burning tobacco to the helper spirits, unrolled the Medicine Bundle, applied a special remedy to the old woman's chest, and began to sing and pray. The other men lifted the dying woman in her robes very gently onto a litter and joined in singing the ancient songs, while slowly proceeding up and down the length of the longhouse.

This unique home structure represented everything that the Haudenosaunee culture stood for: communality, sharing, cooperation, and equality of power between men and women. It was fitting that her body be carried in a symbolic way along this transit that had supported her life for so many years. As the men sang, they danced and shook the rattles and rhythmically beat the drums, all the while summoning their Orenda (higher powers) and directing it into the body and spirit of Kajijonhawe.

After the carrying of the litter was complete, the Elder was again gently placed close to her family's fire pit, wrapped in her robes, where she slept peacefully through the remainder of the night and into the day. Powerful singing could be heard throughout the longhouse village for many hours, songs such as:

Da onen di' eskenongohden' nengen'ne'
gaya'dag'enha' se'awaadon'
onenh enwadongoh'da' nengen' skenon' nen-
gen' onsahenonhdonniyon'

> Translation: So now, moreover, I shall sing to this one to help her, as the Creator said, so that when the ceremony is finished this one will be well disposed.

Unlike the melodies of Western music, which tend to be longer extended musical lines adhering to the length of a verbal sentence or long phrase, the songs of the longhouse were supported by steady pulsing rhythms: reflective of heartbeat and breath cycle, the sounding of crickets and cicadas. The musical phrases were shorter, emphasizing the intervals of fourth and fifth, injecting the closer second interval to balance out the sound architecture. This musical form allowed for powerful output of breath in a regular, emphatic rhythm, followed by deep inhalation in preparation for the next short phrase. By and large, the rhythms were steady, in a meter of four (the earth number), repetitive, like the cycles in nature, with occasional syncopations appearing here and there. This was the music heard in Haudenosaunee dreams.

We are fortunate today to be able to still hear this powerful music in old field recordings made by curious ethnomusicologists in the early years of the twentieth century. My own precious copy of these recordings is in the form of cassette tape and still played on an old tape player. What remains of these ancient songs has been digitalized by the Smithsonian Institute, where they are catalogued and available for purchase and study. Just as exciting are the efforts of modern Haudenosaunee people on the Awkwesasne Nation in New York to remember and revive their ancient songs and ceremonies.

But let's return to Kajijonhawe's medicine ceremony more than five hundred years ago, because it is still sounding beyond the long night and into the daylight hours. Many more songs were cast, songs invoking the animal spirit helpers, songs about throwing piercing objects to effect healing, songs of gratitude. The thirteen men of the Little Water Medicine Society led the singing, amplified by all the women young and old. Alternately dancing and resting, making space for others to take up the rhythms and potent invocations, the energy of healing was raised to a degree of great intensity which permeated all who attended, all in service to their beloved dying Elder. And when Father Sun emitted its last light in the western sky, Kajijohawe took her last shallow breath and her spirit was released to the new road of her dreams. But the songs did not end there—

For the following week, after Kajijonhawe's body was hung in the trees to decompose over the next year, voices were lifted in the *Hai-i Hai-i* chant, a high and piercing wail symbolizing a spirit in flight. The power of this sung-prayer coaxed and ushered the spirits away from the earthly life so that they would not wander aimlessly and confused, only to frighten those who remained with the appearance of their bright white balls of light. The Seneca believed in and often experienced the reality of ghostly presences and were eager to avoid the fright.

Finally, once every ten years or so, the Great Feast of the Dead was held. It was then that all the collected bones of the many decomposed bodies of that decade were buried communally, just as they had lived, with a final send-off of song, dance, drumming, and feasting. A great celebration was officiated by the women, the *gantowisas*, to remember the ancestors and to remind the People that their own spirits would be taking the same journey before too long. *Hai-i!*

FIVE

FRENCH SINGING MONKS

I CAN ALMOST REMEMBER THE FEELING. My French Canadian grandmother, Beatrice, Meme, would hold me close to her warm, ample bosom, working the rocking chair, and singing softly, *"By o By, Do de Do, By o By, Do de Do."* That feeling of comfort, safety, love, ease, warmth, soothing vibration was just the medicine I needed as an infant whenever I felt distressed. We all continue to need this feeling, though sadly, its delivery to us is not assured.

I was my Meme's first of many grandchildren, and the love and pride she must have felt at my arrival was directed into my little body with great tenderness. I know she did this for me because I saw it reenacted by her for all the babies that followed. She was the first Musician Healer I ever knew. She, along with every other woman in history who has administered this kind of motherly, soothing energy and sound to stressful babies, were Musician Healers.

Meme's mother Celeste sang and rocked; Celeste's mother Bibianna sang and rocked; Pelagie, Marie-Joseph, Genevieve, Marie-Marguerite, Perrine and on and on down the matrilineal line, all sang and rocked.

Through the long French Connection, I carry this medicine within me and will throughout my life. *Merci beaucoup ma Meme, et toutes des Memes.*

In 1880, twenty years before Beatrice was born in French Canada, an unusual and interesting medical research paper was published in France, written by a researcher named Diogel who practiced and studied medicine at the Pitié-Salpêtrière Hospital in Paris. I can imagine the derision he would have suffered from skeptical colleagues. Thankfully he carried on with his work, taken up by others into the twentieth century.

Diogel devised a soot-coated drum with a stylus to record patients' vital functions such as cardiac output, respiratory rate, pulse rate, and blood pressure. He then recruited musicians to play live music at the bedsides of his patients in his research lab. After collecting data from numerous trials, he concluded that soothing music lowered blood pressure, increased cardiac output, slowed pulse rate, and generally relaxed the physical body. His findings were later explored by others, notably Dr. James Leonard Corning in America and Tarchanoff in Russia. Did you know that Alexander Borodin, famed Russian composer, was one of the musicians who played at the bedsides of Tarchanoff's patients? Borodin's scientific interests merged with his musical interests, leading him to experience the role of Musician Healer in a hospital setting early in the twentieth century. An early interdisciplinarian.

Jacquet and the Great Abbey

Much earlier, many centuries before Diogel's experiments, the powerful effects of music, not only on the physical body, but on the emotions and spirit, were fully understood and employed by a group of Benedictine monks at the Great Abbey at Cluny, Saône-et-Loire, France. Their story is fascinating. Let me begin by introducing you to little 7-year-old Jacquet, a poor peasant boy who lived in the countryside of Burgundy in the year 1060 with his tenant-farmer father, Papa Claudin and his mother, Maman Maud, along with an older sister and brother. We find little Jacquet playing outside in the door yard, drawing pictures in the sandy soil with a stick and singing a song he learned earlier in the summer, from the Jongleurs who visited his hamlet, entertaining the countryfolk with dances, songs, juggling, and magic tricks. He remembers it as the best day of his life. The Jongleurs recited the story of a great French battle hero, Roland, whose bravery is legendary. The music they played on panpipe, drum, and finger cymbals was jolly, and the song they sang, *Salve Regina*, was so beautiful, Jacquet bound it to memory and joyfully sang it every day.

But on this particular morning, Jacquet quietly wept as he sang the Latin words *O clemens, O pia, O dulcis Virgo Maria.* Reaching out to sweet Mother Mary, he desperately tried to remember a feeling of happiness to thwart the terrible sadness and despair that filled his cruck house that morning.

The previous night, his dear Maman Maud had died during childbirth. So far, his new baby sister had-survived, but was very weak. Jacquet would never forget his beloved Maman's cries as she pushed the little infant out and poured her life's blood onto the bed. When she finally became quiet, Papa Claudin's wailing filled the deathly silence. Jacquet remembers turning over in his bed and muffling his ears with a pillow. His life was about to change.

A week later, Maman was in the ground. His sickly infant sister was placed in the care of a cousin who was nursing her own newborn. Papa Claudin sat with Jacquet and told him that he would soon be brought to the Great Abbey at Cluny, where the monks would teach him and take care of him.

Jacquet's young singing voice was high and clear, and the great Abbott Hugh welcomed him as a gift to the abbey, in exchange for prayers for Maman Maud's soul. As a child oblate, Jacquet was a gift to God. Papa Claudin's responsibilities as a single parent would be lessened.

Three weeks later, Jacquet continued to cry and sing himself to sleep on the small cot in the boys' dormitory. He missed his mother and all his family, and could not understand why he had been sent away. Since his arrival, he hadn't spoken a word, lost in his trauma. But Sweet Mother Mary finally heard his prayers and sent him a ray of light one night as he lay awake, waiting for sleep. A kindly monk, Frère Perpetuo, quietly approached with a lit candle in hand and sat by his bedside. Perpetuo told Jacquet that he would be his special master—would watch over him and teach him. Then the monk began to sing *Salve Regina*. Jacquet stopped crying and listened. And then he joined in with his own sweet voice, a tender beginning of a life-long friendship.

From that night on, Jacquet's days were filled with lessons in French and Latin. He joined five other boys

Abbaye de Cluny, Cluny Abbey.
From the collection of Musée Carnavalet

in his dormitory at the crack of dawn to attend the Hours of Prayer and Chanting, at Prime, followed at three-hour intervals by *Terce, Sext, None, Vespers*, and *Compline*. At each Hour he stood close to Perpetuo, following his every move and tone. Before long, he could rely on his own strong memory and spoke and sang the rituals on his own.

Jacquet was a quick study and his lovely voice added to the great beauty of sound that echoed off the domed stone chamber of chapel. He was filled with awe and newfound happiness, as his days became an ever-repeated round of prayer and music. How wonderful to be able to sing, and sing, and sing. The magic of this new life was healing the trauma that nearly buried him at his arrival to this wondrous place. Sweet Mother Mary feels like his new mother, one who will care for him in the absence of his own dear Maman. Along with Frère Perpetuo. He finally feels safe and loved.

Death of an Elder

In 1060 France, Salvation Economy was a way of life. Catholics, the rich and powerful, and poor alike, concerned for the ultimate redemption of their sinful souls, gifted the monasteries that propagated throughout the country with lands, money, food, and goods—even with children. In exchange, the monks prayed and sang ceaselessly for those souls who shared their wealth, large or meager. The greatest abbey of all, Cluny Abbey, became enormous and lavish as a result.

For hundreds of years, donations poured in,
so fearful were the people for their souls after death.
Cluny Abbey became the most magnificent abbey
in all of Europe.

In the year 910, William I, Duke of Aquitaine, its original benefactor, endowed the first Abbott Berno with a rich foundation of land and money to begin erecting magnificent structures for worship, housing, *infirmaria* for the sick, and libraries for all the music and manuscripts. For hundreds of years, donations poured in, so fearful were the people for their souls after death. Cluny Abbey became the most magnificent abbey in all of Europe. The monks lacked nothing, and despite their vows of simplicity, silence, and celibacy, they lived very comfortable lives indeed.

One late morning, while Jacquet and the boys were receiving their lessons, a loud clattering startled them out of their concentration. It was the sound of a wooden tablet being struck by a monk from the *infirmarium*, announcing the impending death of an Elder Brother. Jacquet looked to the others in his confusion, as they all jumped up out of their seats and headed for the door, running. *Was there a fire?* he wondered anxiously. The teacher grabbed Jacquet and told him to run as fast as he could toward the *infirmarium*, instructing him to chant the *Credo*. This was something completely new. At all other times, the boys were forbidden to run in the cloister. Why could they run now? But he was delighted at the opportunity to fly full steam ahead, as any child would be.

As he ran alongside the others, he sang *Credo in unum deum patrem omnipotentem factorem celi et terrae* (I believe in one God the Father Almighty Creator of Heaven and Earth) . . . the same long prayer I learned by heart as a young Catholic girl nearly one thousand years later. Jacquet was surprised to see every single monk running from every part of the abbey toward the *infirmarium*, brown cassocks fluttering around their feet, all of them chanting the *Credo*. What a strange sight in such an ordinarily quiet and contemplative place.

As they approached their destination, everything slowed down again, and the boys were led into the building single file, Jacquet at the end of the line. They were ushered off to one side as the entire community of monks, including Abbott Hugh, the priests, the *Armarius* (librarian and director of all high rituals) encircled the bed of a very old brother who was nearing death. "Actively dying," is how modern practitioners would describe what the medieval monks would call a "last agony." Drastic changes in breathing, unresponsiveness, mottled extremities, hands pulling at the bed linens, all the same signs that the *infirmarium* workers would look for, we still look for today.

The Credo continued. Followed by a Litany to the Saints. This is how the boy was introduced to the Cluny Abbey death ritual, the direst spiritual emergency of the religious community—a theatrical, musical, and prayerful ritual that surpassed all others in complexity and pomp.

To usher a beloved monk's soul over the threshold to the afterlife was the highest calling of this community of psychopomps—the creatures, spirits, and angels who escort newly deceased souls from Earth into the afterlife. It was the psychopomps' job to convince God to heal and admit this soul through the Pearly Gates; and they did this by being *virtuosi* of sacred prayer and song, pleading for redemption and forgiveness. In this way, the brothers took great spiritual care of each other.

The several days that followed the death were just as ceremonial, leading to burial within the walls of the abbey. Careful preparation of the body followed, always accompanied by chant and prayer, a group of brothers always in the presence of the corpse until the final grand processional from St. Mary's Chapel to the graveyard. Every bell in the abbey rang continuously throughout, declaring the final release of a soul to the glory of God. And all the while, monks lifted their strong voices in song-prayer to the heavens. What an amazing vibratory experience that must have been.

Jacquet was thrilled by the pageantry of this long event, but more so was moved by being present at a death, recalling Maman Maud's final agonies. He was struck by how different this death was. The old monk looked peaceful, without pain or distress, as he was filled with the beautiful music surrounding him. The boy had felt peaceful too, without fear. It was a wonderful, healing thing; a beauteous feeling that would revisit him countless times during the many death rituals that were to follow throughout his long life.

The years passed. Jacquet grew in stature and knowledge. His sweet boy-soprano voice awkwardly changed (some frustrating months of singing) into a rich baritone, now ready to join the choir monks as a fully fledged member. It was a happy day when he joined their ranks. His relationship with Perpetuo had deepened too, and though the two monks were forbidden to embrace, the energetic sphere that surrounded them was full of love. Many more years of studying, singing, and praying together—and yes, laughing and struggling—transformed them into the truest of brothers, the younger and the old.

As was the custom, when Perpetuo's body and singing voice became too weak to continue his active work as a monk, after calmly but tearfully confiding to Jacquet that it was his time to die, he announced this realization and purpose to Abbott Hugh. Abbott Hugh then called all the members of the community to the Chapter House to receive the news, followed by a beautiful ceremony of absolution, forgiveness generously given to and from the dying monk. Jacquet and another brother then led Perpetuo to the *infirmarium* where he asked to be anointed with holy oil for the sick. He was then carefully placed in a bed and lowered close to the floor, so that all his brothers could convene in a circle all around him.

Thus began the sacred liminal time, when Perpetuo finally exhaled a sigh of relief in response to the loving care that would guide him and his soul through the dangerous journey of finding its way back to God. Much like the Bardo of the *Tibetan Book of the Dead,* the monks believed it was a time when the seductions of demonic forces threatened to capture Perpetuo's attention and steer him off the path to God. So the community rallied its own forces with antiphons and the singing of psalms, to overpower the intrusion of evil influences.

Communion was then administered to the dying man while he was still conscious and able to swallow. The priest presented Perpetuo with the crucifix so that he might adore his Savior once more with a kiss. In a moving procession of farewell, each member of the community, including the children, approached their dear Elder and offered him a kiss. Jacquet was last in line, his tears flowing, and as he approached the man who saved him in this life, he quietly sang the *Salve Regina*, and placed his lips upon Perpetuo's brow.

They prayed: *Cor contritum et humiliatum, deus....;* "Do not spurn a contrite and humbled heart, O God, but according to your great mercy, be merciful to him." They then sang the several Psalms of Absolution: Psalm 50, *Miserere mei deus...*; "Be merciful to me, O God, according to your great mercy. And, according to the plenitude of your compassion, wipe out my iniquity...."

They sang and sang, and as they sang, Jacquet realized that his dear friend had fallen into a deep sleep of peace. And the young monk was relieved.

The dying took time, long into the next day. But at all times, Jacquet was allowed to stay at the bedside in vigil, with others. They continued to pray the Litany of the Saints, the *Credo*, and sing through the *Psalter* over and over again. All was softly lit in candlelight. It was a time outside of time. The healing power of the moment could not have been greater. When Perpetuo's shallow respirations were finally spaced by longer and longer periods of quiet, one of the monks, well-versed in the signs of imminent death, picked up the wooden tablets and raced to the dormitory, where all were asleep. When Jacquet heard the clattering arousing his brothers, he was suddenly flooded with memories of all the times he and Perpetuo had run like the wind together to usher another soul safely into heaven. Singing and praying, always singing and praying. It was time to let go.

The weeks and months that followed Perpetuo's death were full of sadness and grief for Jacquet. Not unlike what he had felt as a small boy after the death of his Maman. But whenever he lifted his voice in song and prayer, a warm medicine filled him with strength to go on, and he was again healed.

SIX

RAGA

I WAS A YOUNG WOMAN in the late 1960s, listening to the popular music of the day, when I first heard the glorious classical music of India, raga, played by the great musical ambassador Ravi Shankar. I was mesmerized. Beyond the awe I felt in response to the seemingly superhuman virtuosity displayed on his instrument, the sitar, I was equally amazed by how focused and calm this man remained while executing some of the most complex melodies and rhythms I had ever heard. This was powerful stuff.

It was also at this time that I was a sophomore in college, taking a required course in public speaking. I needed a topic for my next assignment and decided that I'd do a little research in this fascinating musical form and talk about it to my classmates. It was simply a brief presentation of the fundamentals, but my discovery nevertheless remained with me as an example of extraordinary musical expression. It's now more than fifty years after that early exposure, and raga reappears, after all that time, as the perfect addition to this book about the deep past of music and healing. Isn't it fascinating how the past remains alive in us, incubating sometimes for many years, before reemerging for further scrutiny and understanding? So let's take another look and listen, with older eyes and ears.

The young student of Western music begins with *do re mi fa sol la ti*. I remember well learning *solfeggio* (the reading of music using these note names) when I was a girl in elementary school. Sadly, this kind of sound literacy is no longer universally taught in schools, a huge loss. I was fortunate. In India, a young student of classical Indian music, raga, begins with *sa n ga ma pa dha ni*. Ah, seven notes again, so both systems have something in common. In addition, both systems use sharps and flats within the seven-tone scale, adding five more pitches to the sequence, so both begin with a sound palette of twelve tone possibilities. But beyond this similarity, raga takes off on an interstellar sound trip which goes way beyond the stretch of Western music, as we know it.

Nada

Central to the understanding of raga is the concept of nada. Nada means 'sound' in Sanskrit. But not just any ordinary sound. Nada is the primal sound, the source of all creation. Perhaps nada is actually the sounding silence, from which all other sounds emerge. Indian music as it first appeared more than six thousand years ago is based on this original, sacred sound. And because of that, the Divine is at the heart of all Indian music. This inner potency gives raga its particular ability to influence the minds, hearts, bodies, and spirits of its listeners. Something that Western music can also do. But given the fact that this divine sound practice has been developing since 4000 BCE, always backed by an awareness of its sacred component, raga employs a particularly powerful effect on people, so much so that its use as a therapeutic tool is unchallenged. Sadly, Western music does not yet enjoy such universal acceptance as medicine. But our music is so much younger, in comparison. Things take time.

Indian raga employs a particularly
powerful effect on people,
so much so that its use as a therapeutic tool
is unchallenged.

In 4000 BCE, Indian music was based on just a three or four note scale. Verses from the Vedas, India's ancient sacred scriptures, were sung to these simple melodic fragments. Plainchant comes to mind, a much later but similar Western liturgical musical form. But as raga evolved, more and more tonal territory was explored, so that not only more whole tones and halftones were included in the scales, but also microtones, tiny fractions of halftones. Music in all cultures is based on pitch or sound frequency, as well as spatial relationships between pitches. The way in which pitches are arranged, one after another, creates melody. Add rhythm to the mix, and you have music. What is fascinating about Indian music is its complexity. A much larger variety of frequencies are employed in raga, compared to Western music. And the complicated polyrhythmic patterns which bring this music to life make Western music seem simple by comparison.

Music is all about numbers. It is a highly evolved artistic form of mathematics really. Each pitch or note can be measured by its number of sound waves per second. Add just another sound wave or two to the original pitch, and you have a higher microtone. Subtract a bit of sound energy, and you get a lower microtone. It is nearly imperceptible to our ears, and yet Indian music is full of this subtle play on pitch. Rhythm is all about divisions of a simple pulse or beat. Melody is a linear shape created by subsequent notes separated by varying spatial intervals. Mathematics appears in various ways throughout musical structure and theory.

When we compare the numbers reflected in both Western and Indian music, we begin to understand how Indian music seems to be playing with a fuller deck of sound possibilities. The number of basic scales in the Western system is thirty, by my count: twelve major scales, twelve minor scales and six modes (major or minor scales with characteristic spatial alterations between one or two notes). Indian music, on the other hand, is based on seventy-two principal scales, which employ many micro frequencies which live between the whole and halftones of Western music, thus enlarging the pitch vocabulary. Indian scales are also differentiated by other nuances, such as ornamentation and dynamic emphasis of one note or another. Using this vast array of possibilities, the seventy-two principal scales of Indian music can be expanded to create seventy-two thousand ragas, each a distinctive sonic representation of color, mood, emotion, energy, and state of being. Of course, it doesn't end there. Because raga is improvisational music, based on just one of these seventy-two thousand tonal formulas, the number of artistic performances which can be derived from this vast resource is infinite. Think on that.

Raga Chikitsa and Healing

One has to wonder how Indian musicians put this kind of sonic power to use. Perhaps recalling my vision of Ravi Shankar playing raga on the sitar will be a good place to start. Remember how I noted earlier how calm and focused he appeared as he enacted musical feats of great technical difficulty? Picture him sitting comfortably and solidly on a cushion, his body upright, breathing slowly and deeply, a serene look on his face, while cascades of rapidly sounding notes, obeying some unearthly polyrhythm, float outward into the atmosphere. No strain, no tension, just pure free expression, while his body/mind/spirit appears to hold a state of perfect equilibrium.

What I've just described is the state of whole health and wellness, which can lead to the ability to access great power. Shankar achieves this state while playing the sitar. But how does his music affect those who are listening to it? As I write this, I am listening to an audio recording of Shankar playing "Raga Kausi Kanhara." I can only imagine what it might feel like to actually be in his presence while playing. The experience, I expect, would be heightened and refined, since it would not be buffered by the electronic medium which delivers it to my ears and being. But for now, I can report that within a few minutes of listening, my focus is sharpened, my breathing is easy and regular, a feeling of buoyancy is developing within my body. As he repeats and reinforces the primal tone of the raga, which is C# (432 Hz, also known as the "Ohm" frequency), and adorns it with his improvised use of the other tones in the raga sequence, often bending tones, the rhythms gradually become more and more intricate, and the pace quickens. I can feel those energies rising easily within my body, all the while remaining calm and focused. The pulse is incorporated within me, and I begin to move and dance gently while seated.

It takes many years of study and practice to understand, not to mention play, Indian classical music. My understanding, as presented here, is very limited. But what I do understand perfectly well is that musical performance, spiritual uplift, and healing are never separated in this tradition. Each raga is associated with a time of day, a physical element (earth, air, fire, water), a planet, an astrological sign, a chakra (energy center within the body), a nadis (nerve center). In this way, the Hindu belief in relationship among all things is demonstrated and utilized.

Raga Chikitsa is the application of raga for healing purposes. And this practice works beautifully in tandem with Ayurveda, the ancient Indian medicine which is still administered today. Similar to the other historic cultures we've already looked at, herbal medicines are coupled with spiritual devotion, yoga and breathing practices, and various forms of music (instrumental and vocal) to bring about therapeutic effects. The entire person is treated: body, mind, emotion, and spirit. I can attest to the holistic effect created, simply by listening to "Raga Kausi Kanhara" for fifteen minutes. My body feels refreshed, my mind and emotions are calm, I feel well-balanced and uplifted.

A man in modern-day India, named Sri Ganapathi Sachidananda Swamiji, who has studied and practiced Raga Chikitsa for many years, has catalogued numerous ragas he has used to treat various illnesses. For instance, Raga Sandhya Kalyani is effective with ear, nose, and eye diseases. Raga Ranjani is effective with kidney disease. Raga Madhuvarshini is good for nervous disorders, headache, sleeplessness, and sinus problems. He utilizes the specific frequencies prevalent in each raga to re-balance the chakra and nadis energies related to the disease. Through resonance, the power of these sonic frequencies is taken on by the body and a healthier equilibrium is achieved. But it is not simply through exposure to sound that these healings are affected. It is Sri Swamiji's own state of being and focused intention, coupled with an openness by his patient, that catalyzes and compounds the effects even more. In this way, the body and mind and spirit all take part in the process and a healthier whole is achieved.

Cultivating Wholeness

We who would wish to develop our own skills as modern-day Musician Healers should consider all these elements as we develop our own work. Cultivating one's own wholeness through serious life-giving practices, strengthening our commitment to helping others, developing a focused way of directing good intention, relying upon help from unseen forces, and refining our musical capacities to go beyond the sphere of artistic performance. All these factors played an important part in the healing practices of each of the ancient cultures in this series of chapters: Ancient Egypt, North American First Nations, France in the Middle Ages, and Indian raga that goes back to ancient times. Musician healers of today need all these qualifications, and others, passed down to us from the healers of long ago, if we hope to do our best work.

PART TWO

TECHNIQUES & ILLUMINATIONS

INTRODUCTION, PART TWO

THE MAKING OF A MUSICIAN HEALER

"You are not a drop in the ocean.
You are the entire ocean in a drop.
Seek the wisdom that will untie your knot.
Seek the path that demands your whole being."

—Rumi

I MAKE BREAD. I do not set out to bake unless I have free, open time. My bread comes out best, and is most delicious and nourishing, when I am physically calm, well-rested, and feeling in good emotional balance, as I put it all together. While I knead the dough, I think of nothing else other than injecting all this good energy into the mix and motion. After the double rising, I open myself to enjoying the wholesome aroma that fills the house during the bake. As I remove the loaves from the oven, I feel the satisfaction of having made something beautiful. And then, after brief cooling, I butter the first warm slice for myself and thoroughly enjoy eating manna. If others are present, they get to enjoy it too.

This is such a perfect metaphor for what it's like for me to make music as a healer. As musicians, we are makers. What we make contains all the energies we put into it. If the energy that we generate and channel is of the highest quality, then what we make is of the highest quality. When an artistic creation, music, contains energy of the highest quality, it can be a powerful force for healing. A true Musician Healer has the ability to inhabit her Mystery Body while making music. In this way she can transform art into medicine.

When we musicians are 'well-tuned',
the quality of our own energy changes.
It is strengthened, clarified, balanced, focused,
and very powerful.

As highly trained musicians, we have spent many hours and years of practice on our instruments. We have repeatedly played scales, technical studies, études, musical pieces, all the while perfecting physical techniques which address posture, finger work, hand positions, various physical movements (depending upon instrument), sound dynamics, rhythmic control, tone painting, phrase shaping, extended line shaping, larger form shaping, and so much more. All this, and more, we do until a work of art emerges in a coherent, expressive, and hopefully beautiful form. Sounds hard, doesn't it? And it is. Becoming an accomplished musician is a very long opus based on commitment, patience, and years and years of work. But if you aim to be a Musician Healer, this is barely the beginning.

Wow! Could there really be more? You bet. And the 'more' is this: unless you are truly ready to look deeply inside and take on the great task of knowing, understanding, nourishing, and transforming yourself into a channeler of powerful energy that can truly heal people on all levels, physical, emotional, and spiritual, then your music will find its home in the world of art (a fine achievement in itself), but will not cross over into the realm of healing potency.

Here we venture into the territory of Energy: forces that are unseen, but deeply felt. Although science has found ways to measure various forms of energy, thus validating its existence (in a materialistic sense), the practice of 'Energy Medicine' is still considered *woo-woo* by many who have not opened themselves to experiencing its powerful effects.

Well, I say, "Free the Woo!" And let's start calling it by a respectful name so we can move on and take advantage of all the bounty Energy Medicine has to offer. Musician Healers will be ambassadors in this important effort. Every time I can deliver healing energy through the sharing of music that is created by a Self that is calm, clear, well-intentioned, and full of heart, is one more opportunity to show the world one particular way of practicing Energy Medicine. And when those applications lead to obvious positive effects for those receiving it, there is more qualified evidence of its power to heal.

Consider this: we musicians are actually instruments playing our instruments. My piano tuner is here right now, tuning my grand after a long, hot, humid summer. I am lucky to have a fine Yamaha Conservatory Grand which tenaciously holds a pretty good tune through thick and thin. But after my friend leaves this afternoon, the piano will be smiling, gleaming in its bright and balanced newness of sound, and I will play Rachmaninoff tonight, just for myself, for my own bliss.

When we musicians are 'well-tuned', the quality of our own energy changes. It is strengthened, clarified, balanced, focused, and very powerful. This requires tending to our physical health, our emotional and mental state, and our spiritual connection. It requires living a full and rich life, practicing creativity in any way that appeals to us, nurturing loving relationships, both with ourselves and others, and practicing a peaceful and contemplative way of being in the world. If we do this faithfully, whenever we sit down to play, we will be channeling our very best energy into our musical instrument. The potency of combining two well-tuned instruments, musician and piano (or any other instrument), is remarkable. That's when music can become medicine.

SEVEN

STATE OF THE BREATH

OUR LIVES AS INDIVIDUALS, just released from the womb, begin with one simple yet very profound act: the inhalation of breath. For the first time, a great gulp of oxygen is delivered to our tiny lungs, then throughout our bodies by a physical action not dependent upon mother. As though startled by the immensity of this experience, we then exhale the unneeded component of carbon dioxide (in addition to a small amount of oxygen and lots of nitrogen), our first act of letting go, and cry out our declaration of autonomous being, "I am here!" We are inspired and animated by this most visceral event. We are finally functioning within the rhythm of life on our own.

A fundamental element of spiritual/religious philosophies throughout the world, and throughout time, is the Breath. For example, the inhalation/exhalation cycle is symbolic of Taoist belief, the balance of opposites which is the yin and yang of all life. That first breath cycle is our initiation into the world of movement and pulse. It's not only oxygen that fills our bodies when we inhale but spirit itself. Without spirit, the essence of life, we would not be animated beings in the physical world. Consider the roots of words such as inspire and expire. The Latin word for breath, *spiritus*, encodes the close relationship shared by breath and spirit. Upon birth, we are inspired, and as we exhale our final breath at death, we expire. Spirit enters our bodies at birth and leaves our bodies at death. We enter and exit this life through the same gateway, the Breath. Our physical bodies, while alive, are vehicles for something quite powerful and marvelous. During our lifetimes, we circulate a sea of air that enriches and enlivens our physical bodies, while it continuously re-injects spirit into our beings. How amazing is that?

Perfectionism and Inner Insecurity

Several months ago, quite by surprise, I took on a 11-year-old girl as a private piano student. I had not taught piano, as such, for many years. But hers was a special case, and it seemed like the right opportunity to return to private teaching, even while I continue my clinical healing work in hospitals and nursing homes. Lana's early life had been peppered with emotional trauma, poverty, and lack of resources.

Lana had been the center of a custody battle between her mother and grandmother, and now that her mother had regained custody, she was doing her best to provide Lana with special supports to help her deal with emotional outbursts and difficult behavior. A local church had stepped in to provide financial help in the way of a musical scholarship to pay for piano lessons for this child who had shown a particular interest and talent in music. When her mother discovered that I was both a therapist and teacher, she

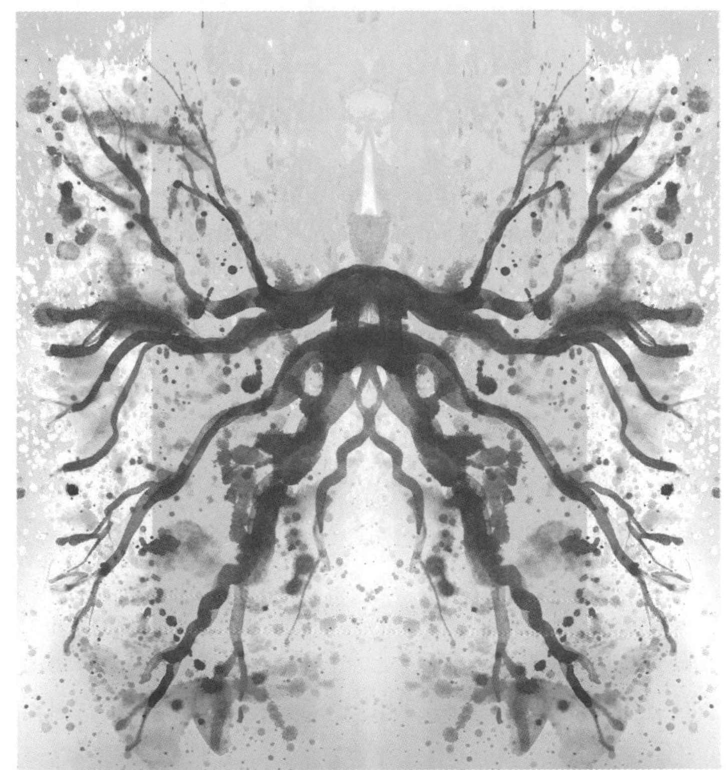

ILLUSTRATION: RICH THÉROUX

We enter and exit this life through the same gateway, the Breath.

asked me to work with her daughter. I couldn't refuse, knowing that Lana might benefit from all the healing components I would bring to bear in her musical experience.

So we began. It soon became clear that Lana was very bright, truly loved music, and struggled with the need to never make mistakes. Perfectionism within a young being tends to be founded on inner insecurity, a fear that one has to be perfect in order not to be rejected by those she depends upon. I know this emotional territory well, as it was a strong feature of my own childhood. While it can lead to great achievement, it also brings with it enormous stress and tension, and can develop into all sorts of psychological disorders and much unhappiness. It was necessary for me to address this immediately with Lana so she could be freed from this dangerous predicament.

As we worked together to find middle C, her little hand's first position at the keyboard, and then on to read the notes of very simple tunes, we also practiced deep breathing. Whenever she made a mistake, she typically held her breath, sputtered a verbal excuse, and tried to plow ahead, only to make more and more mistakes.

I could visibly see her beating herself up for failing. I told her, "Lana, it's good that you are making mistakes. That's how we learn. Let's learn to giggle when that happens, and then to stop and take a deep breath before we begin again." I also asked her to take a few deep breaths before playing, teaching her how to more fully and audibly exhale, reminding her that her brain needed good food (clean oxygen) and her muscles needed to relax.

Over time, she has learned to do this more often on her own. It is the simplest of instruction, and a habit that can be cultivated in short time, with gentle guidance and repetition. Now when she plays, I notice her taking deep breaths during difficult passages, on her own. This girl is on her way to not only better piano playing but a new and healthier way of being in her mind and body.

Working With the Breath

I was in my mid-twenties when I first began working with my own breath. This was in the 1970s, when Eastern spiritual philosophies and practices were being introduced to an American counterculture, open to radical change. I discovered that yoga and meditation were ways to access my inner world, something that many Scorpios like myself are drawn to. The simple instruction of Transcendental Meditation, to simply focus on the breath, sparked my curiosity, and it was then that I committed to practicing deep and free breathing on a daily basis.

I struggled at first to break the long-held pattern of shallow chest breathing that had been firmly planted over the years within my body. But over time, I noticed that the soft muscles in my belly loosened, my urge to tuck in my tummy weakened, fresh air was more regularly reaching the lower parts of my lungs, and this was happening more often without my full awareness. This changed my life. I now had a better way to deal with stress, maintain calm, and improve general health. My mind was clearer. And, as an extra special bonus, I could adapt this practice to the piano keyboard where my playing became freer. After more than fifty years of practicing this way of breathing and being, it's impossible to describe how deeply and wonderfully this has affected everything I do. It truly has.

Many of us are unfamiliar with the practice of deep breathing. I learned from the yogic system of *pranayama* which teaches how to regulate breathing using a complex system of exercises. Hindus call the invisible essence of life *prana*, which is delivered via the breath. *Prana* invigorates us, clarifies and concentrates our energies, helps to focus our minds, and makes it possible for us to access deeper and higher states of consciousness. *Prana* is not spirit as such, but a close cousin, as it is a very powerful and invisible energy force. Learning how to regulate the breath through deep breathing is the one best physical practice you can acquire to improve and sustain good health throughout your entire life.

Prana invigorates us, clarifies and concentrates
our energies, helps to focus our minds,
and makes it possible for us to access
deeper and higher states of consciousness.

Trained singers and players of wind instruments are already at an advantage here since breath is the fuel that fires their musical sounds. But the rest of us, keyboard, string, percussion players, may not have spent much time considering the importance of breath in music making, much less within our daily lives. So, let's begin simply by learning the most fundamental exercise of *pranayama*: how to easily and efficiently inhale the most clean air that our lungs can accommodate, followed by a long and slow exhalation which empties the lungs as fully as possible. This type of breathing is sometimes called diaphragmatic or belly breathing.

First, let's take a look at the anatomy involved. When we inhale, we draw air in through the nostrils (and sometimes the mouth, but for purposes of this exercise let's use only the nostrils). It flows through the throat and on into the lungs. As we pull the air in, the diaphragm muscle, which sits directly beneath the lungs, contracts and lowers its position to open up more room for the lower parts of the lungs to expand with air. If this muscle contraction is working properly, the abdomen will be pushed out, making more room for the diaphragm to slip down. In this way we can fill the lungs with as much air as they are capable of receiving.

When we exhale, the diaphragm muscle relaxes to its original higher position, the abdomen returns to a more normal inward position, and all the air is automatically pushed out, leaving the lungs clear of unneeded elements and creating a vacuum which makes it easy for the next inhalation of air to automatically rush in. At this point in the cycle, we can experience the return of the diaphragm to its more upper and relaxed position by tucking in the abdomen with slight pulses of energy. Doing this helps us to feel the workings of our anatomy in a more sensual way.

Basically, breathing is a process of contraction and relaxation, filling and emptying. Muscles and space are involved. We can more vividly and viscerally experience air, or *prana*, coming in and going out of our bodies. And we learn how to control that flow in order to receive the best benefit.

Most people breathe in a very different and shallow way. The bottom parts of the lungs are rarely used.

Instead of using the diaphragm to help draw in more clean air, the shoulders rise in an attempt to pack more air into the upper lungs. This actually has little or no impact on increasing the volume of air since the upper lung has already taken in as much as its space will allow for. When we become stressed, we sometimes shut down the cycle completely, holding our breath, which is the worst thing one can do in that situation. A much better alternative is to breathe deeply and efficiently, which supports relaxation, clear thinking, and energizes our bodies with *prana*.

A good way to practice is while sitting in a straight chair or standing with legs evenly spread in a balanced position. Back straight, head forward, place the palms on your solar plexus just above the abdomen. After breathing in your normal way a few cycles, on the last exhalation, push as much air out as possible through the mouth, blowing it through pursed lips. Now close the mouth and draw air in through the nostrils. As you do this slowly, push the lower part of your torso out using your muscles to do so, and allow the air to be drawn into the lower parts of your lungs. When you are filled, exhale through pursed lips, pulling the abdomen inward which releases the diaphragm, until you feel emptied. Repeat this several times. It may feel quite awkward at first, but don't give up. Practice this for only five minutes or so, then return to it another day. No reason to rush. The more you practice in a moderate way, the easier it will become.

After you get the hang of the movements involved, you can add another element to the practice. Inhale on four slow counts, hold the breath for four slow counts, and then exhale on eight slow counts. The aim is to extend the exhalation period to fully experience the feeling of letting go and relaxing. If you allow it, the lungs will empty themselves and be ready for the next round of clean air. Breathing deeply and well is, simply put, working and resting, working and resting. Pulling in, letting go. Yin and yang manifest in the physical body.

Spiritual Energy

Breathing comes into play in a big way while I'm working as Musician Healer. Unlike the above exercise, I do not usually need to exhale audibly through the mouth, unless I notice a buildup of tension within myself. For the most part, there is nothing unusual about the way I look as I breathe. Even though deep breathing is now an unconscious mainstay of my everyday life, an even fuller awareness of my breathing cycle kicks in as I enter the door of the facility or home where I am to interact with a person who needs help. I remind myself that the breath will stay with me throughout the session, both as my own physical body and mind support as well as a carrier of *prana* and spiritual energy.

As I approach the person or family I'm working with, continued deep breathing helps me to slow the process down, to take my time as I talk with and listen to them. Spaces of silence are allowed, which give us all a time to rest and consider. I often notice that as time passes, the breathing of others in my company may change subtly, from shallow and quick to a little deeper and slower. The calmer energy I bring with me into the room has a noticeable effect on others, and when the change manifests itself in the way in which I notice them breathing, I know that good medicine is happening.

When I begin to play or sing music in this setting, the deep breathing always continues. It settles me into focusing on the music I am making, keeps my mind fresh and my physical muscles relaxed even while they are working. The breath also helps me to easily and fluidly divert my attention to the patient, even while playing, so I can notice the effects that the music is having on his or her state of being.

Breathing fully and well supports conservation of energy and attention, so little is wasted on unimportant things, like stress, negative self-talk, confusion, protective defenses. It allows me to stay very open to what is happening, at the time it is happening, and to respond accordingly in a helpful way. The music I play and sing also benefits from the steady infusion of deep breath. It is delivered from a place of inspiration and healthy energy and as a result is more beautiful. If I were playing in a concert hall, I would use my breath for the same result, but here in this healing setting I can be assured that the music I offer as a medicine will be the most beautiful I can make in that moment. This has a very powerful effect on listeners—their attention is held in a state of suspended receptivity and the stress of illness, worry, fear, or helplessness is momentarily put aside. Music played in this way draws those present into a higher level of experience which can provide a much-needed break from the hard work of being sick or caring for the sick.

There is no better example of the essential power of the breath than my way of working at the bedside of one who is dying. Unless one dies suddenly, from an accident or a massive medical crisis like heart attack or stroke, dying is a process that takes time. If one is dying from serious disease such as cancer or naturally from old age, the decline is often gradual until a physical threshold is crossed when we say that the person is 'actively dying'. At this point, death is nearing but there is another shorter process to get through. We notice that the person's breathing pattern begins to change. Because major organ systems are breaking down, less oxygen is required. Inhalations sometimes become more rapid and shallow. It appears that breathing is more labored. Eventually the time period between each inhalation/exhalation cycle lengthens. Often mucous builds up in the breathing passages to create a gurgling, congested sound which is referred to as the 'death rattle'. This stage is in some ways similar to what a pregnant woman goes through during the last stage of birthing a child. It is a major piece of work and a time when support and guidance is needed and useful.

My thoughts and actions at this point are preoccupied with the fact that the person's spirit, housed within the breath, is working hard to leave the physical body which can no longer sustain life. I often sing quietly very close to the ear, exaggerating my own breathing so that my cycles of breath are audible. Breathing while singing, especially while singing slow and gentle songs, requires deep inhalations and long exhalations, the same kind of deep breathing that leads to relaxation, calm, and regeneration of energy. When I'm not singing, I will continue breathing in this way but simply place a single audible tone on the out-breath, so the person will continue to hear and feel the rhythmic cycle which my breath is creating. In many cases, before long, the more struggled breathing pattern of the dying one will change and become a bit more relaxed. The long periods between breaths are no longer fraught with tension but become periods of suspension when the physical body practices floating without the life force for a little while, to become accustomed to the new terrain. If a patient is slow to respond to this way of working, I will change my own breathing pattern to match the more strained cycle of the dying person. Sometimes my breaths will be quick and rapid, sometimes more shallow and broadly spaced.

With this technique, I can join the person where they are in their process, and then lead them into a more relaxed pattern as that becomes easier for them. Sometimes this takes hours. At other times, a person is just ready to go and we can achieve this transition in a matter of fifteen or twenty minutes. Finally, when all is ready, the last inhalation can be taken and given up in a very natural way. The spirit, the breath, flies away, and the body is at last free to rest. Like the birth of a child, it is another kind of birthing indeed.

What's important to remember is that music itself breathes, doesn't it? The rhythm and flow of music is much like breathing. Whenever music is interjected into the mix of therapies, a special sonic sort of breathing reinforces the positive outcomes I hope to bring into a situation. Music with a regular pulse, periods of repetition, suspension, and resolution, along with pleasing harmonies and gentle melodies, helps to support the regulation of physical breathing, heart rate, blood pressure, and cranial sacral pulsation within the human body. As I play or sing, my own physical body is balanced, followed by the bodies of my patients and others who are attending. This kind of healing is a communal experience, which can create a loop of calming energy which regenerates itself and is passed back and forth among us. After I've worked in this way for an hour, the environment itself is often charged with soothing vibrations which can linger for some time.

Spiritual Helpers

This morning I heard Faure's lovely *Pavane for Orchestra* on the radio. Music like this is a perfect backdrop for creating an experience of peace and ease. Whether from an electronic audio source or played on an acoustic instrument such as piano, an artistic rendering of gentle, deep breathing adds a powerful ingredient to any healing practice which aims to soothe the body and mind and alleviate suffering.

I'll briefly mention here that the breath is also a vehicle I use to summon the help of spiritual entities. I don't work alone. These unseen spiritual forces that come into play are less easy to identify or quantify. However, my personal awareness of spiritual helpers is ever present, regardless of whether or not my patient is oriented to this sort of experience. They are my allies in this work, and their contributions to the tasks are indispensable to me. I am fortified and strengthened in confidence by my teamwork with them, and am ever-grateful that all I need do is breathe deeply and summon their presence to have them at my side. My actions in difficult situations often feel mysteriously guided by such forces. Things I might not see clearly on my own are at times revealed with little effort on my part so I know how to proceed. I most often feel quite energized and light when leaving an hour of deep work, an indication that much of the load was carried by my spiritual team. Little do my patients and families know that I arrive with an army of co-healers, but I do. And as I continue to breathe deeply and fully throughout my days, even away from my healing work, they accompany me everywhere and lend a helping, healing hand. We'll explore this more mystical way of working later on in the book.

For now, let's keep it simple. Consider practicing deep breathing, starting very gradually to bring it into your daily lives for manageable periods of time. Then put it away, give it a rest, and return to it again with fuller awareness. Be patient and give yourself plenty of time to experiment with these new physical sensations. Bring it with you into your musical practice, and discover how it affects your playing, your clarity of mind, your freedom of expression, your enjoyment of the process. And when you share your music with others, whether in a private informal setting, on a concert stage, or at the bedside of someone who needs your reassuring help, bring the Breath along with you as your friendly, helpful sidekick. You may be surprised by the enormous and wonderful difference it makes.

EIGHT

THE GENEROUS HEART

THERE IS NO BETTER REMEDY for what ails you than feeling one's pain, hard as that is. A broken heart catalyzes acutely sharp emotion, brings deep understanding of our human condition, is instrumental in powerful healing, and often is revealed in beautiful art.

You may think it a bit strange that this is where I begin thinking and writing about the Heart. Perhaps it is because that is the course my own personal life has followed. My childhood experiences were overshadowed by broken hearted-ness, and I see my long life as the story of putting my heart back together again.

The Sacred Heart

A religious image I remember seeing repeatedly during my early years was that of The Sacred Heart; Jesus wearing a red robe which was open at his chest, revealing his heart as a flaming organ, wrapped in thorns and pierced by a sword. It symbolized the immense love that he was capable of showering upon us. The fruit of his suffering was compassion. Powerful stuff, indeed. The mystery of the potency of pain, loss, and defeat was understood intuitively, even by my child self. I had already lived through some of that, and it hadn't killed me. In fact, it has served as a reference point all these years, as I continue to face the variety of life's pains, all the while strengthening my abilities to create and heal. My brokenness has tenderized my heart. I've come to understand that there is no richness of life, no deep inner growth, unless one has suffered and learned how to work with that. Life is indeed boot camp for the soul.

One of the strongest threads that binds us
as living creatures is the pain of living,
and I want to be able to fully share
in that bond with everyone.

To my mind, our North American culture focuses too much on enjoyment, success, and avoiding difficult stuff as much as possible. Look around you and notice how people often paste forced smiles on their faces in a desperate attempt to keep things going smoothly? Everybody seems happy. The problem with that is we lose a lot of learning, and spiritual and emotional strengthening, by pushing away the awareness and experience of pain.

Openness to pain actually relieves suffering. When I encounter a pasted smile on someone's face, I see a deeper internal suffering that continues to fester and grow if the pain isn't acknowledged, named, felt, and eventually released. This life was never meant to be a bed of roses, though the great irony is that once one embraces the full measure of feeling, making room for pain seems to eventually amplify the sensation of joy. Having learned this, I've become one of the more content people I know. And still, from time to time, I weep from a very deep place in my heart. It seems to me, that is the most honest and healthy way to move through my life. It also provides a continual emotional workout for the most central of energy centers in our beings, the heart chakra, keeping it strong and resilient and ever more powerful.

How often do you cry? Do you remember how often you cried when you were a child? As the most essential muscle in our physical bodies, isn't it odd that the only way we feel compelled to exercise the heart, as adults, is through aerobic exercise? That's all fine and good, but what about practicing regular emotional fitness?

I've recently enjoyed the great relief that only a good cry can give me. I notice that I am more deeply touched by the experiences I have with my patients and doing my work as Musician Healer. When I feel emotional pain, I can more freely express it. And therefore, my own suffering is diminished.

Sharing in a Bond

One of the strongest threads that binds us as living creatures is the pain of living, and I want to be able to fully share in that bond with everyone. It humbles me, softens me, honors my vulnerability, and makes me a better healer.

Of course, the heart center is capable of much more than just being shattered, and thankfully so. Falling in love registers very high on the list of 'High-Heart Joys.' The sexual and amorous attraction we feel toward another human being enlivens the heart, makes us feel totally alive and full of energy. Let's add to the joy-list the way I, and many of us, can feel around our children and grandchildren; the loving connection we can feel in the beauty of nature; the fullness we feel while enjoying a work of art or music; or the feeling of peace and power while in a spiritual state. These joyful heart feelings are so completely opposite to the feelings of loss and brokenness that it astonishes me how wide is the range of energetic possibilities of this organ, chakra, and energy center we call the Heart.

The HeartMath Institute is a research and education organization conceived in 1991 to explore the powerful effects a strong heart intelligence can have on one's sense of well-being, connectedness with others and the world, effectiveness in one's work, and potential for human growth. Their research has shown that the heart, like all systems within our bodies and beings, does not operate in isolation. Rather it is directly connected to the workings of our minds and emotions. The heart and brain communicate neurologically and continually. They have found that the heart's communication with the brain far exceeds the amount of communication the brain has with the heart.

We all understand how central the brain is to all the physical, mental, and emotional workings of our selves. We often think of it as the main switchboard within our bodies which controls all the essential

ILLUSTRATION: RICH THÉROUX

The Heart is directly connected to the workings of our minds and emotions.

life-giving processes and systems, such as respiration, blood circulation, hormonal production and distribution, the digestive and excretory systems, the immune system, and so forth. Brain death means death to the total human being. Given that, think of how direct information from a healthy heart center into that brain might affect the general performance of a heart-evolved being in a positive and powerful way.

Now, I'm not just talking about caretaking the heart with ample exercise, healthy diet, plenty of rest, and good management of stress, as important as all that is for continuing good physical health. I have gone deeper into heart territory to understand how nurturing the heart center by implanting it with feelings of love and compassion can positively affect the workings of every other system within our beings. Our minds become clearer, our intuition grows stronger, our respiration deepens and eases, our brains communicate more effectively with each life-sustaining system including our immunity, when our hearts are fed with and generating love. We feel better in general, and we operate more effectively within our relationships and lives.

Getting in Touch with Our Hearts

So how can we get in touch with the working of our hearts, beyond being heartbroken or falling in love, in a way that helps us to be evolved Musician Healers? First we must know how to love ourselves, and that's a big undertaking. I won't explore this until later in the book. Just know that learning to truly love others won't be possible without this. But let's put that aside for now. The big question we must ask ourselves is: How do I see and relate to others, especially those in my care as a Healer? Am I able to see everyone I encounter as a being who is lovable? I realize that I am setting a very high bar here. And my honest answer to this question, for myself, is "No, not always." But I'm working on it, and the more I work on it, the more I am able to put aside my defenses and petty judgments in order to see something closer to the essence of a person. This is so worth doing, believe me.

ILLUSTRATION: RICH THÉROUX

A strong and open Heart intelligence can improve one's sense of well-being, and connectedness with others and the world.

I've worked with many different kinds of people over the years. Some endearing, others less so, and at least a few who seemed ugly to the core. Just imagine the variety of people you have encountered, and had to deal with, in your life. It's natural and right that we are drawn to certain personalities and avoid others. We need not be enduring friends with everyone. Personally, I am acquainted with lots of people but I can count my closest friends on the fingers of one hand. But that doesn't stop me from opening my heart to others in a way that asks that I be present with them, even for a very brief time. This is a practice. It must be intentionally done, prepared for, every time I'm about to walk into a patient's room or greet a group of Elders in wheelchairs, patiently waiting for me to start playing the piano.

Much is made these days of 'Mindfulness.' Focusing our attention on the present, as we pass through it and into the next present, is another practice that helps tremendously in the hard work of opening up to people. It's quite enough to have to deal with one moment, each little event, as we flow down the stream. One little thing at a time, slow and steady wins the race. Taking in more than a moment at a time complicates things, often adding anxiety, self-doubt, defensive emotions and postures that come from our past experiences, some of which are painful and threatening. The people I work with are often burdened by such defensive emotions and postures, and it's my job to not add to the mix my own. Mindfulness helps me to keep my energy clear.

Broken Hearted-ness

None of us escapes broken hearted-ness in this life, and much of that begins in early childhood. Gabor Maté, a wise therapist and educator, talks and writes about how the manifestations of mental illness and even everyday ineffectiveness and stress in dealing with our lives and others, all stem from the defensive compensations we have made within ourselves as a result of painful experiences in childhood. I believe this to be true. Not one of us has escaped broken hearted-ness as a child. It comes in so many forms and ways, ignores social, economic, racial status, is evenly distributed to both girls and boys alike. It's simply a function of being in this world and living in the midst of other people who have before experienced their own versions of broken hearted-ness and who have usually unwittingly inflicted some of their own pain on us.

Some people have enough resilience and character, support and resources, to work their way through and beyond such unhealthy compensations. But it often takes a lifetime to make strong headway, and even then there still remain blocks to total openness extended to others. I gratefully see myself in this group of people who have made some progress with this, which has made it possible for me to do the work of reaching people from a deep and less-complicated place. That place is the True Heart. So the next step beyond mindfulness, for me, is heartful-ness. I move from the workings of my mind (which certainly feels like it is housed in my head) to the workings of the Heart (which is a distinctive, visceral experience within the center of my chest).

There is no better example of when I feel the warm opening of my heart than when I am in the presence of my granddaughter. My younger readers will not yet know the wonder of this, as grandparenting is a distance away in your lives. But when it eventually hits you, you'll know it for what it is: an undeniable miracle in the life of an older person. When young Olivia crosses my threshold, the warm love in my chest lights up and fills my entire being. There is no holding it back. It's instantaneous and powerful. Her young, sweet, innocent energy mingles with my energy, and the happiness of our connection makes me want to give everything of my best self to her. That's love.

Generous Giving

Generous giving is a hallmark of deep love. The gift is an important metaphor in describing just how we enact Heart-centered love. Indigenous Peoples, most notably those from the Pacific Northwest region, such as Kwakiutl and Nootka, practiced (and still practice) a ritualistic form of giving called the potlatch, which is from the Chinookan word *Patshatl*. Families who were celebrating an important event, such as a marriage or birth, would gather with their community and give away lavish gifts to mark their own joy and good fortune. Unlike our more modern and familiar practice of receiving gifts when celebrating such landmark events, these Indigenous People found it quite natural to share with others many precious possessions, sometimes nearly completely diminishing their personal resources as a result. Besides being occasions that demonstrate wealth and prominence through the giving away of goods, the trust they must have felt in the inevitability of others sharing reciprocally with them, in love and celebration, must have been substantial.

So what is it that I have that is most precious to me? What are the very best gifts I might bestow on those I love—not only young Olivia, but most especially to those I work with and wish to heal, in whatever way that might be possible? My best self gives away my time, my focused attention, my patience, my acceptance without judgment, my fearlessness in the face of strong emotions, my calm yet strong energy, my careful listening, my honest response. I offer all these gifts to my granddaughter, which is such a good way to practice offering them to my patients. Bestowing this kind of energy upon others in my care often elicits healing in a variety of forms. Good energy is good medicine.

There is one more very precious gift I offer to others. And that is my music. As musicians, I think we can all agree that our musical talent and expression are among our most precious personal treasures. For me, they are at the top of the list. It's while making music that I feel like my most put-together, whole self. It's when many parts of my brain light up, creating a sense of wondrous balance in my being. It's when I am broadcasting my best and clearest energy. So, what better gift to give away?

The music give-away is not a performance. Conservatory training, and the conventional world of art, emphasize performance. I think of performance as, *Let me show you what I can do.* In this modern world, we are thrilled, entertained, and impressed by artists of all kinds who perform with great virtuosity and exceptional skill. Indeed, an immense amount of money is exchanged while commodifying great art (and too often less than great art). Our finest artists are glorified, idolized, mythologized, and perhaps even burdened by fame.

When I was a child, I was occasionally pressed by my parents to sing or play piano for visiting guests. I hated it, to the point of sometimes backing away and sulking. I felt uncomfortable with being put on display. I didn't like the gushing accolades and attention, and felt as if I were being placed on a pedestal above everyone present. I often thought, even as a young girl, *Why can't you just let me do what I do without all the fuss?* Don't get me wrong. I appreciated, and still appreciate, that my creative expression was, and is, appreciated. But I was discomfited by the excess of attention, being singled out as exceptional. Although at that age, I didn't know the word, nor its meaning, I realize now that I felt 'commodified'. What I truly wanted, and needed, was to be part of humanity, not elevated above it. I found that pedestal to be a very lonely place.

My consciousness transforms what might otherwise
be called 'performance' into the more
joyous state, for me, of 'Healing'.

It has taken me many years to find a way to share my music on my own, comfortable terms. Giving my music away while embodying a full and generous heart is the way I choose. The fact that I am monetarily compensated for my work does not change the sensibility of 'give away'. Holding that sensibility firmly within my consciousness transforms what might otherwise be called 'performance' into the more joyous state, for me, of 'healing'.

So how do I act out this loving generosity in my work with people? I do not set any particular agenda other than to provide beautiful music infused with calm and compassionate energy and directed with a clear intention to help. I recognize that my listeners are people who carry burdens. Many of them are living in facilities that, although providing good care, will never take the place of being at home. Homesickness is a real malady, and I see it often.

Many are bearing physical pain, which, managed to some degree with drugs, never completely goes away. It is a nagging ache that robs them of the freedom to place their attention on things that bring pleasure and joy. Many suffer from dementias which lead to confusion and fear, sometimes aggression, as if acting out in violence can release them from the emotional and mental entrapment they are living. Many are actively dying, perhaps fearfully, perhaps with acceptance. But either way, dying is a piece of work that must be done essentially alone. As one heads into the unknown of what comes after life in the body, every ounce of courage is demanded when physical energy is waning steadily, unrelentingly.

I think about these things as I walk through the door and know that I cannot change m any of the realities they are facing. But I approach them bearing gifts. I bring to them my calm, strong energy. I bring to them an open, compassionate heart, one which allows me to feel a little of what they are going through and to just be with that. I bring to them the most beautiful music I can make in that moment, willing the sound to carry whatever medicinal and healing effects each might need, trusting that I don't need to always know what those needs are, trusting that what will help will be provided.

The effects of receiving energy from a compassionate heart are specific, and even measurable. For my readers who want more scientific evidence, a clinical study on the effects of focused compassionate energy on human beings was conducted by Kathi J. Kemper and Hossam A. Shaltout and published in the official journal of the International Society for Complementary Medicine Research, BioMed Central. The study is titled "Non-verbal communication of compassion: measuring psychophysiologic effects." Subjects were measured for levels of stress, relaxation and peacefulness, as well as respiratory rate and heart rate variability, before and after the experimental exposure to compassionate heartfelt energy. An experienced practitioner of loving-kindness meditation (a non-verbal way of communicating compassion) was placed in a room with each subject for four, 10-minute intervals. To maintain blindness, the practitioner and subject were instructed to simply read a book quietly. In this way, the subjects were not aware of the practitioner's intention to communicate compassion in their direction. Both parties were equipped with monitors measuring various physiological activities (heart rate, respiration, skin temperature).

The measurements gathered and analyzed at the experiment's conclusion revealed significant reductions in the subjects' level of stress (2.2 vs 5.5) and respiratory rate, and increases in levels of relaxation (8.8 vs 3.8), peacefulness (9.0 vs 3.8), and heart rate variability. This study used the Visual Analogue Scale (VAS) which is a subjective self-report measure consisting simply of a 10 centimeter line with a statement at each end representing one extreme of the dimension being measured, most often intensity of pain.

Calm and Compassionate Heart

The quality of the energy which we as Musician Healers send out to our listeners affects the energetic experience of those within and close to our field. The work must always, always begin within ourselves. If we bring relaxed, peaceful, compassionate energy to the making of music and the sharing of it with others, we will see remarkable healing effects such as those revealed in the scientific study, and, I will add, many more effects which are less easily measurable: elevation of mood, reduction of fear and anxiety, stepping out of isolation into connectedness, sometimes reduction of physical pain and certainly reduction of emotional pain.

Your calm and compassionate Heart is indeed one of your strongest allies and tools. Tend it well, use it often. Now let's move on to the power of intention and all the magic that can be activated by developing this amazing power, which remains dormant in many of us until we wake it up.

NINE

THE MAGIC OF WILLFUL INTENTION

MAGIC HAS ALWAYS BEEN and forever will be. When my daughter was little, and learning how to speak, she would say: "My mommy is a magician." She meant to say musician, but the workings of her little mouth and tongue could not yet pronounce that word correctly. I rather liked her version of things. Through the years her pronunciation and pronouncement have actually been realized. I am a magician as well as a musician.

The Oxford American Dictionary defines magic as "the power of apparently influencing the course of events by using mysterious or supernatural forces." I've discovered that I have the capacity to create outcomes by using my powers of intention and will. We all have that potential, but not everyone is ready to explore this. It takes a long time, a lot of soul evolution and growth, before one is equipped to explore this magical terrain. What makes it 'mysterious and supernatural' is only because so few in today's world have realized this power and practice it. Someday hopefully, human beings will have evolved to claim the magic and put it to good use. But before that happens on a grand scale, I suggest my readers begin by considering it a possibility.

We actually use the power of intention every day of our lives. We get up in the morning, decide to shower, eat breakfast, and manage to accomplish these things with little trouble. We've become so accustomed to being able to act out what we decide to do that we lose sight of what a little miracle that is. Of course, the simple decisions of each day are relatively easy to make, so habitual are they. We just put our minds in gear, make a silent intention to carry something out, and then act. It all happens in a moment's passing. In many cases, we are not even mindful or aware of the process as it unfolds.

Then there are harder decisions to be made. Should I go out tonight with my friends, or stay home and get the extra sleep I need to fight off a cold coming on? Should I trade in my car now and take on an extended car payment, or let my vehicle run out its life course and risk more repair bills? Should I write a letter to my estranged brother who has been avoiding me, or accept the loss of relationship? These are decisions which take careful thought since they lead to eventual consequences which are not always predictable. Setting an intention to act may take more time and care to craft.

I use intention in my healing work all the time because I have found that practicing it with clarity of mind in my daily life, whether my decisions are big or small, helps me to attain the results that I want.

Clarity is the key. Refining one's purpose and focusing on that target narrows the aim. What would be more important than using the power of clear intention in my work which can lead to important consequences and results for those in my care? This leaves me with the big question, every time I prepare to encounter a patient or a group, what is my intention?

As performing musicians, your broad intention may be to entertain your audience. A more focused intention may be to move your audience on an emotional level. Perhaps you are in a competition and your intention is to play your best. As a Musician Healer, my broadest intention is always to do no harm, to help. Filtering that down a bit, I intend to bring strong and calm energy into an environment. A more specific intention may be to calm and ease anxiety or discomfort within my listeners. While working with the dying, I aim to support the elevation of spirit from the physical body through the application of sound and music. Or even more specifically, to ease and regulate a difficult breathing pattern. Relieving anxiety and discomfort goes without saying. For people with advanced dementia, my intentional focus is to capture their attention and bring it into the present moment. Or to draw them back into memories of youth and vitality. And, in a pinch, when I may not know specifically what is needed in any situation, I carefully focus on delivering whatever it is that is needed. This will cover a lot of territory that I may not see and will truly address whatever is most needed. This is the 'default intention,' at all times. I don't necessarily have to know the particulars; I just need to intend to deliver whatever is necessary. This works particularly well in a group situation, where individual needs will vary.

The point is, placing these intentions clearly within my mind before I deliver the medicine of sound and music, is essential to realizing an outcome. If our thoughts are scattered, our intention will not be clear. Vietnamese peace activist Thích Nhất Hạnh said it well:

> Breath is the bridge which connects life to consciousness, which unites your body to your thoughts. Whenever your mind becomes scattered, use your breath as the means to take hold of your mind again.

If we breathe into our bodies, our minds, and then through our heart chakras, our intentions will be grounded in compassionate caring. Incorporating breath, thought, and visualization of intent in this way is a potent preliminary to achieving good results.

Tuning the Energy Field

I often incorporate breath, thought, and visualization of intent as I walk through the doors of the various facilities where I work. As I do this, I tune the energy field that emanates from my being, which has a resonating effect on those with whom I come into contact. It takes little time, once you've practiced it for a while, and can have a big impact on refining a musical sharing experience into an effective healing experience.

But that is only the first half of the process of musical magic. Take a moment and place your hands on your solar plexus, the area of your torso just beneath the rib cage. Get a sense of how this is the center of your body, a deep core of energy. Kundalini yoga names this *manipura*, the third chakra. It's also the location of the diaphragm, the muscle I mentioned earlier that relates to the expansion of the lungs during deep breathing. *Manipura* is translated from Sanskrit as 'lustrous gem'. The energies associated with this chakra are fiery and golden yellow. It is the seat of our will and power. When we practice deep breathing, we exercise this chakra and help keep it healthy and clear. Our sense of confidence, faith in our abilities, and self-esteem are all strengthened. It becomes more and more natural to believe and witness that which we intend to accomplish.

We can learn to direct our intended energy through this chakra. The image of an archer comes to mind: standing erect and solid on the ground, with feet spread and balanced, the archer lifts the bow, sets her sight (the intention), deeply inhales, and pulls back the stringed arrow, then releases the breath and fiery energy, hitting her target.

When I'm working with people, making music while remembering my intentions, I can imagine the sounds and energy being sent out toward my targets. My *manipura* is actively engaged in this process, though the only way I physically experience this is while I am breathing deeply at the keyboard, and while I sing. My body, my mind, my spiritual energies are all working in sync. It's interesting that the artistic quality of the music I make also improves. What's otherwise difficult can feel effortless. I notice that even if I am playing a less-than-wonderful piano, somewhat out of tune (this is sadly too often the case), I can still make it sing—at least enough to make it beautiful for my listeners.

The effects that this way of sharing music has on others is consistent and powerful. To me, this is magic of a high order. But if you still think that magic is just the stuff of fairy tales, consider this quote by the French philosopher Henri Bergson:

> Some are born with spiritual immune systems that sooner or later give rejection to the illusory worldview grafted upon them from birth through social conditioning. They begin sensing that something is amiss, and start looking for answers. Inner knowledge and anomalous outer experiences show them a side of reality others are oblivious to, and so begins their journey of awakening. Each step of the journey is made by following the heart instead of following the crowd and by choosing knowledge over the veils of ignorance.

I'm with Henri. Although Bergson's philosophical writings predate us by a century, he was able to free himself from the accepted beliefs of his day because of "inner knowledge and anomalous outer experiences" which countered what was conventionally accepted as truth. I have witnessed so many anomalous experiences in my work, that I know, without a doubt, that the power of intention and will are real. Real magic.

TEN

I DO NOT WORK ALONE

I've alluded earlier to the company I keep, the spiritual company that is, while I'm working. It's how I live my life actually, so bringing spiritual company to work is natural. It's a strategy to help ensure that I'll do my best work. I can't do anything that's really meaningful and powerful all by myself. That's hubris, that would be my ego at work, and ego gets in the way of being able to let in all the dynamic, energetic help the universe and its helpers have to offer a small soul like me.

This is true for all of us. Whether you subscribe to a traditional religion or spiritual practice or follow your own unique way of working with the mysteries of the universe, we all can depend on our spiritual helpers to boost the power and effectiveness of our work and lives. We also need their presence to support us in maintaining our own personal health and healing powers. This is a big job, and it calls for a team effort.

My most immediate helpers have names. I know their names because they told me. I suspect and sense that I have a big crowd of helpers, more than I can count, but the ones that show up most, and which I call upon most, are a small group of faithful companions.

Their names and identities came to me through the years in the same way my own name, Runningdeer, came to me—through a spiritual/psychic transmission that was clearly audible to my inner ear and vividly experienced as a physical incident, many years ago.

When I was 25 years old, I lived with my young daughter in a trailer in the woods of southern New Hampshire. We were poor. I'd been through a brief early marriage and a couple of difficult relationships with men. My daughter had just started first grade in the rural public school, and I had my mornings free to myself. Lost as I felt and was, I began meditating each day after putting my child on the school bus. After meditation I walked through the woods to a small open meadow which bordered a stream. When I reached the meadow, I would pray, sometimes out loud, to the nature spirits which I felt came alive. Sometimes I chanted. And often I simply stood quietly to listen to the sounds of the trees and water, the breeze and birds. I followed the same path every day, without fail, always feeling pulled and welcomed by the ever-growing powerful energy which was building up over time. After retracing my steps back home, I would sit and write in my journal. I was learning and realizing important spiritual truths, and recording them was a necessary part of my practice.

Becoming Runningdeer

One day, I repeated my usual practice of venturing into the wood. It was autumn, the woodland smelled pungent and damp. The early morning sun was still rising in the sky. As I stood quietly in the meadow, I was suddenly overcome with a sharp sense of danger. My breathing quickened as I listened more carefully, looking all about. Without a second thought, I turned and ran as fast as I could back down the well-trodden path toward my home, toward safety. As I ran, I was infused with the Spirit of Deer. I felt that I had become a deer. And to this day, I wonder if anyone else had been around to see, would I have actually looked like a deer? Perhaps. First Nations shamans call this shape-shifting, and I was blessed with this powerful initiating experience at a time in my life when I was devoting so much energy to understanding who I really was, and what forces I could depend on to guide me through difficult times in my life. I was given the spiritual energy of the deer: a keen sense of awareness, a swift response to danger, the wisdom to quickly retreat when trouble is near; also her grace, her strength and power to clearly discern. The memory of that event is seared into my heart and soul.

A few days later, still shimmering with this infusion, I received a crystal-clear message to my inner ear. I felt the presence of an Indigenous grandmother, and she said "Runningdeer. Your name is Runningdeer." I immediately began telling my close friends and family that my new name was Runningdeer. I had long carried the names of men, my father and divorced husband, feeling like I was wearing a coat that never fit right. It was time for the coat to finally come off. And although some people couldn't understand this sudden change, some even ridiculed me, my closest people did understand. I have been Islene Runningdeer ever since. My new coat fit perfectly.

Musicians' Helpers

My helpers have names too. They are St. Thérèse of Lisieux, a special spiritual guardian of my mother and all her children; Red Cloud, brave Lakota chief who came to me in the early days; and Pretty Flower, an Indigenous grandmother who tells stories, laughs a lot, and who sometimes gently chastens me. There is also Big Hawk, who I may once have been married to. He accompanies me, most especially, with his masculine strength and help when I approach people to bring them music medicine. Finally there is my mother, Doris, ten-years deceased but still very easily accessible. Behind these primary helpers flock hundreds of others whose names I don't know, but whose presence I feel. I sense they are always with me but they become all-the-more present when I consciously call upon them.

You have helpers too. I believe they are there, whether you know of them or not. If you wish to meet them, just make yourself available. Ask them to make themselves known so you can be more familiar and comfortable in their presence. You will need them if you are serious about bringing your music and energy to help others heal. You cannot do this alone.

The world is in pretty bad shape, and its people are suffering in so many different ways. If as a musician you feel called to bring balm and strength to its weary travelers, now is the time to think about your own spiritual understanding of existence. If you haven't yet fully done this, let me be your guide. Maybe I can think of some good questions that we should ask ourselves in order to get to the heart of this.

Perhaps you have no interest in looking more deeply into the meaning of everything we see and sense and experience in this lifetime. You may have no belief in a God or Higher Power, and subscribe to a totally rational, scientific point of view. If so, then the role of Musician Healer is not for you. But to those of you who sense that something great and mysterious and in some broad sense, Divine, is transpiring all around us (even though you may not yet have a clear understanding of it all), in this chapter and the next, let's think about these questions:

Who is God? What is God?
Who/What am I?
Why am I here?
What happens when I die? Where do I go?
Where have all the ancestral souls gone?
Do I pray? How do I pray?
Is there a higher calling for the artist/musician?

I'll attempt to answer these questions, for myself, to set a template for readers to work with. I expect that our answers will be different, since each of us is an individual with our own unique experience and understanding. But I also expect that we might find some common ground here and there. My answers are not meant to be your answers. Just food for thought.

I'm struck by how big an assignment this is and am preparing myself for some deep digging and perhaps some surprises along the way. So, let's begin.

Who is God? What is God?

'God', in my estimation, is simply a name for a power or energy which is unnameable. Whether the name used is God, Allah, Buddha, Yahweh, Great Spirit, it's just a name that is not the real thing. We humans are limited by brain, intellect, and language in our attempts to understand and describe 'The Divine', which is just another name. A name I sometimes use to reference the unnameable is 'Source'. I think of Source as being the origin of all that is, all that is seen and unseen, and all that was and ever will be. But the name Source doesn't suffice, indicating the origin or beginning, because I suspect that there never was a beginning, nor will there be an end. Living in our linear timescape, it's more than difficult to imagine and experience the infinitude of that idea.

When I was a child, I thought about such things. A mind game I liked to play was contemplating the idea of zero. I vividly recall the day, while taking a walk after school, that I understood the paradox of zero: that the concept of zero denoted nothing, while the concept of zero was itself something. I reasoned, in an instinctive algebraic way, that, *if nothing is something, then something is nothing.* This equation helped me to experience, to sense, the infinitude behind somethingness and nothingness, if that makes any sense.

It was a feeling, a deep sense, of being connected to a power much, much greater than me and my little life. So, in this little life story, words, and mathematical reasoning helped me to achieve a state of realization and understanding. But the words and the math were simply tools of expression that led me to a different dimensional experience, which I have stored within me as a reference point to 'God'. What do you think, or feel, or sense?

Who/What am I?

A few admired heroes of my life start off this conversation nicely. Buddhist teacher Joan Halifax says,

> Our roots stretch back to blue-green algae. They stretch to the stars. The history is inscribed within us. Silence and solitude enjoin us to remember our whole and great body.

Joni Mitchell sang,

We are stardust, we are golden....

Jane Roberts, channeling the messages of a spiritual entity named Seth, declared that,

> We are multidimensional beings living in a multidimensional reality.

Tuning the Human Biofield: Healing with Vibrational Sound Therapy author Eileen Day McCusick says,

> We are electromagnetic beings bathed in an electromagnetically connected reality—all really is One in this very simple way… [3]

These are grand statements, not easy to fully grasp. Even so, I know and accept them as truth. It's easier to start out answering the question, "Who and What am I?" with the more mundane particulars. For example,

[3] Eileen Day McCusick. *Tuning the Human Biofield: Healing with Vibrational Sound Therapy.* Healing Arts Press, Rochester, Vt., 2014.

I am a woman aging into Elderhood (73 years old at time of this writing), a mother, grandmother, sister, daughter of parents now in a different dimension. I am a musician, a healer, a writer, a thinker, a teacher. I am a friend. I happen to be an American, with a recent blood heritage that conjoins the French Canadian and Indigenous Peoples. I am a homeowner, a taxpayer, and a citizen who votes. You get the idea. These are all labels for describing what my current and visible Earthly life is all about. But it just cracks the surface. I'm sure you can come up with your own list of surface identities in little time. They are the easiest to see.

So, what lies beneath all that? I sense that who I am right now, in this lifetime, has been informed by my ancestors. My sister, the genealogical researcher of my family, tells me that besides our French Canadian and First Nations bloodlines, our heritage flows into Scots, English, Scandinavian, ancient Egyptian, Syrian, and Greek blood. I am a product of all their lives. I came into this world with traits, sensitivities, and inclinations which derived from their life experiences. We are connected in this way.

Of course, I have elaborated upon those, made them my own, developed them and put them to my own uses. And I fully expect that those who have sprung from me—one daughter, one granddaughter—are a continuation of all this information embodied. I know it's true, because I see much of my likeness in them, further evolved, configured in a different way.

I am grateful that some of the ancestors I knew, or have been told about, were musical people, were nurses, writers, and hard workers. They worked hard-scrabble farms or lived simple natural lives as woods people. In much deeper history, they were even royalty. My musical gifts, my propensity to heal, my love of nature, my easy ability to write, my willingness to work hard to reach a goal, all these things have been passed down to me through the lives of many others in my human family. What do you know about your ancestry and the lives those ancestors lived? It's an important question, for you are they and they are you.

I feel [divine energy] I know it, it's my gateway
to an ever-expanding and clarifying dimension
of experience that has followed me
and guarded me for the ages.

Deeper still, I am my thoughts and emotions, dreams, and memories.

When I'm very still and quiet, I can encounter something at my core that must be source energy. It feels like a soul, an essence, some form of energy that is constant and infinite. I seem to be able to connect with all souls at this place. I can ask for spiritual and energetic help from other dimensions while seated in this place, and this core is its way in. This core is the stuff of what might be called divine energy. I reach for the words to describe this sense that I have, but nothing suffices. I feel it, I know it, it's my gateway to an ever-expanding and clarifying dimension of experience that has followed me and guarded me for the ages. I refer to this core of myself all the time, in my daily life, my relationships, my studies, my work. As my soul has grown in understanding, throughout who knows how many, or exactly what kind of lifetimes, I've finally come to this 'now' of awareness and power. I've learned how to harness source energy and put it to good use. With more and more practice, this ability will become stronger.

Why is it important for us to know who and what we are? Because that is what we bring to our music and to the world. Our music is infused with all this stuff, it is colored by all our individual particulars. And when we become aware of our very rich and true natures, we can bring the fullness of all that energy into a musical healing experience with others.

Why am I here?

This question is all about meaning. Why should I have to spend eighty-plus years on this Earth, not particularly enchanted with much about modern life in the Western world where I live?

Please don't misunderstand. I find beauty in life, particularly in nature, and within my close relationships. Music and art are a great balm, and humankind's best attempt at making something good. I enjoy musical and artistic creations immensely, but every day, I long for something better than the busy and uncentered culture I live in.

It's not always easy living in a physical body, so that's something else to be endured at times too. I often wish my telepathic powers were stronger so I might beam myself through the great spaces that separate me from loved ones or places I might want to visit. I feel as if I must have already experienced a reality so wonderful and enriching and joyful—somewhere beyond this Earthly one—that this lifetime of mine pales in comparison. Given that, what am I doing here? There must be some purpose to all this messy daily living.

I often feel that I must have taken on an assignment to do something needed while I'm here. Perhaps that's what we mean by 'having a calling'. But my senses tell me that the meaning I'm looking for probably has many layers. I'm not here just for one possibly lofty purpose.

First, I must be here to learn. I've messed up plenty, especially in my young adulthood. I have caused pain for others I love and have loved. I've wrestled with hard lessons, finally accepting the unavoidable fact that I am far from perfect. Having defended myself through a traumatic childhood by striving for perfection in order to be deserving of love and protection, I entered adulthood straitjacketed by illusions of who I was, and who I should be. It was a great grace that I finally confronted my own darkness, struggled through long sickness and suffering, and finally decided to be honest with myself, compassionate toward all my emotions and weaknesses. It was a great lesson that needed learning. One of many lessons, some still in progress.

ELEVEN

HIGHER CALLING

LET'S FACE IT, LIVING HURTS. I've suffered my share but in the end have found that there was always something that needed learning from those experiences. Those hard lessons have ultimately led me closer to wholeness and a capacity for healing others. So, being a student of life is purpose number one. For me that means understanding more clearly who I am, what I can offer others, and then figuring out a way to do it. That's a lot to work on, and learn, in a lifetime.

But why all this learning? The more I learn about myself, the more I grow and change. When I connect with others, the energy I have to offer interfaces with them, giving them a chance to respond and maybe even learn from who I am and how I am.

I'm not just talking about sharing peace and light energy. Potential learning happens for others with whom I interact, even when I'm out of balance, reactive, defensive. That's true for me too when I encounter difficult energy in others. All of us are here to encounter and teach others, whether we are aware of it or not. Each of us living today is participating in a lifelong workshop, to make some gains toward self-understanding and love. Perhaps even enlightenment. I don't understand at all the timelines involved, since each one is following a trajectory and tempo unlike anyone else's. But I sense that we must all be moving forward, even if only at a snail's pace. I'm here, I believe, to help along the small parcel of people I interact with during my lifetime, and likewise to be helped along by them. That's my purpose number two. Knowing this helps it to be okay that I'm here at all.

But back to 'the calling'. My calling has to do with my soulfulness reaching others' soulfulness. I happen to have a talent for music, so that's the vehicle I use to accomplish this little mission. Music is indeed my first language, which I often speak eloquently. I'm here to put my artful talent to use, to teach others how to be calmer and clearer within themselves. I'm also here to advance the world's current and miserly understanding of what music is all about.

Much has been lost from ancient times when the power of sound and music was understood and utilized to heal all kinds of ills. I'm one of the modern-day people whose work is to reintroduce this practice to the Western world. It has been difficult, given the rejection, lack of interest, lack of funding, and near-constant need to legitimize my work. Thankfully, I've had the resilience to keep on keeping on. Though the older I get, the more tired and impatient I've become. I've definitely made some inroads, and I think they will outlive me. I must admit, it has been a big piece of work. So, purpose number three is the goal I originally set many years ago: to bring music back into the world as medicine.

What happens when I die? Where do I go?

My easy answer to this question is, *I don't know!* But I am open to imagining some possibilities. A good friend of mine wrote this poem. I like the mystery and strangeness it evokes—and it brings to mind this hard question, which may be unanswerable until we get there.

You Can Imagine The Difficulties
By C.B.

You can imagine the difficulties
The question itself
Was at first impossible to phrase
Lacking sleep
Away from clocks
The dimension of time
Became the wall of a well
Into which we climbed
Without orders
or expectations
We remained patient
During the descent
The deeper we went
The easier it became
To forgive
Several of us
For several days now
Have been asking for news
Of our own survival

While pondering this question of survival for myself, the poet, whom I shall call Carolyn, is, herself, in the process of dying. At age 77, and without any particular terminal illness ravaging her body, she decided it was her time to leave this earthly plane and has been fasting for the past three weeks. She has her own deep, personal reasons for doing this. Her daughter, friends, doctor, and I support her in this endeavor, without judgment, and have been witness to her journey. She is within a few days of death, ready to slip into coma, pass through a transitional phase of rather dramatic breathing changes, take her last breath, *and then what...?* We know that the physical body will die. But what about the essence, the consciousness, the spirit of my friend?

I have lots of opportunities to consider this question since I regularly sit vigil at deathbeds and deliver vocal music and sound to people who are experiencing the life to death transition that my friend is currently undergoing. So I have witnessed the crossing, the edge if you will, and have been left with impressions.

***

Three little asterisks can denote so much. A day or so has lapsed since last writing, and during that time I spent the last hour of life with my friend Carolyn, her adult daughter sitting nearby as witness and loving support. Sometimes I can maintain a state of balance and clarity in my daily life that draws in the perfect experience, in the perfect time frame. Such has just happened. As I'm pondering the question, *Where do we go?* the amazingly beautiful death of my friend, which I guided with song, breath, toning and tuning fork, presented to me with the simplest of answers. We go to light.

Although I've known this for a long time, have read many accounts of near-death experiences which support its truth, I finally saw it with my own eyes yesterday morning, just moments before my friend died. I'll tell you the story.

A Focused Presence

I arrived at Carolyn's deathbed at 9 a.m. She was very thin of course, ashen in color, and unconscious. Her breathing was rapid and shallow. No signs of congestion building up in her air tract, so I thought she might still be with us for the remainder of the day, perhaps into the next. But I am often fooled. I sat down, centered myself, and leaned in closely toward her head. I spoke: "Carolyn, this is Islene Runningdeer. I'm here to breathe with you and help you move forward. Shall we begin?"

Carolyn could not respond verbally, but I sensed her focused presence. I noticed that she was already exhaling with an audible sound placed on the breath, which told me that she instinctively knew how to soothe herself with vibration. I did not have to teach her that, so I simply joined her, breathing in her rhythm, and placing my own vocal sound on my exhalation. We were toning together, very gently. But still she worked hard to get those breaths into her lungs, harder than she needed to. My aim was to slow things down, which would require deeper relaxation. But we breathed together in her more rapid fashion, without noticeable change for about fifteen minutes, and then I told her that I would back away for a little bit while she processed what we had just experienced together.

When I returned six or seven minutes later, I used a Hemi-Sync [4] audio recording as background music to our breathing practice. I interjected simple verbal instruction, such as "relax," "easy," "gently," all spoken on the extended outbreath.

As she entered this new and final phase,
I noticed spheres of light dancing on the wall,
connected to her body by a
long strand of thin light.

Within a few minutes, her rhythm began to slow. I reinforced this new gait by continuing to breathe more easily with her, toning on the outbreath. After a while, I backed away again so she could continue on her own. With gentle music continuing to play in the background, she held her ground.

After a brief rest, I returned to Carolyn's side and began to sing. Very softly, very slowly, but with deep audible breaths echoing her own, which were now much more relaxed. Her daughter asked for "Thuma Mina," the South African liberation song which had special meaning for her mother. "Blessed Quietness"

[4] Hemi-Sync Audio Guidance Technology, The Monroe Institute.

followed, filling my lungs and the room with more deep relaxation, reflected in Carolyn's demeanor and breathing pattern. I finished with "Now is the Cool of the Day," a song that she loved hearing me sing. We continued to breathe together for a time, I repeatedly exhaled on the word "Free," and then suddenly her pattern changed abruptly. I heard a slight gurgle of congestion in her throat, something that usually happens near the end but continues on for some time. It did not appear to bother her in the least, however, and her final breaths were just little sips divided by long periods of apnea (periods of suspended breathing).

As she entered this new and final phase, I noticed spheres of light dancing on the wall, connected to her body by a long strand of thin light. I gazed at this, wondering where in the room the reflection was coming from, but when I turned to find the source, I couldn't find one. The lights continued to dance in a lively fashion and then suddenly disappeared. That's when Carolyn took her final three tiny, easy sips of breath and took her leave. This entire process took just over one hour, so willing and efficient was she.

Carolyn's lights left her physical body just before the body itself expired. They were generously shown to me. I saw them. I knew she was laughing and free. And she reaffirmed to me that yes, we do go to light.

Beyond that, I do not know. I will find out, in my own time, when it is my time to leave the body and hopefully dance my light on the wall for others to see. What do you think?

Where have the ancestral souls and lights gone? Physicists claim that time stops at the speed of light. Beyond that, there is another dimension. I've been thinking about black holes these days and how light cannot resist the pull into a dark tunnel that is created by the enormous mass of energy that resides inside. Is that where all the light/souls go? Before his death, Stephen Hawking pondered black holes, and where they might lead us. With his genius and finely informed sense of humor, he pondered the big questions, not using the word soul necessarily, but most certainly the word light.[5]

I imagine and wonder if a black hole might be an enormous recycling center. I wonder if it is like the tunnels described by dying people who have had near death experiences—a tunnel that connects a soul that reaches the other end to an awesome light force? Hawking claimed that some energy mass could indeed be spit back out the opening of a black hole, challenging what was originally thought. Is this an expression of some souls returning for reincarnated lives? And do those light/souls who continue on into the awesome light-force on the back-end remain there, in the new dimension, to continue their work of guidance from that place beyond time?

When my mother died, hers was a sudden death. Alone in her room, having just finished dressing for the day, she suffered a quick heart attack, dying instantly. My soulful sensitivity has always imagined that her lights left her body at unimaginable speed and traveled very far. I believe hers was one of the souls that made it to the other end of a black tunnel and beyond, into

[5] Stephen Hawking. Public Lecture "Into a Black Hole," 2008.

that vast and infinite dimension. I call on her lights often to aid me in my life and in my work.

Music can reside in both dimensions, I believe. When I ask for support from my ancestral spirit helpers while playing the piano in a healing capacity, is my music infused with some special light that amplifies its power to heal? And are black holes the route that can connect our physical dimension with theirs?

You may be wondering about my state of sanity at this point. And that's okay. But imagination is what took Stephen Hawking and Albert Einstein and others down their long paths of scientific discovery. If it's all the same to you, I'll continue pondering where our lights go. I've seen them, how they leave our dying bodies and then suddenly vanish—to where?

Do I Pray? How do I Pray?

Growing up Catholic, I learned to memorize prescribed prayers, repeating them verbally or silently because I was taught that I'd better, or else. That ended early in my life when I began to discover my own reasons for and ways of praying.

These days, I pray when I breathe. I breathe in spiritual help and breathe out love. I pray when I sing, in much the same way, breathing in spiritual help, breathing out love. I pray by sounding my tuning forks, directing them toward certain people and intentions. I pray every time I feel grateful for something, and as I get older, this happens more and more. Looking at the sky, walking in nature, swimming in the waters, these all feel prayerful to me. Do you pray?

Is there a higher calling for the artist/musician?
I certainly think so. But it took me much of my young life to realize this. Performance for performance's sake never felt comfortable to me. I've never been one to show off, and I hated when people made such a big deal of me. I shied away from sharing my talents, until I was reminded by a teacher that hiding away my talent was wasting a great gift, a gift that I really had little or nothing to do with. I was just the messenger.

All the most important things I've learned in my life have taken a long time to put together, to fully understand. It wasn't until it finally hit me just how powerfully affected people were when they received my art that I realized how my music could be of great service to others, not for my own glorification, but for their greater good. When that clarity sunk into my bones, everything changed—far less self-consciousness, much freer musical expression, and true enjoyment of my own powers as a musician. Now I give it away freely (though I am adequately paid), and grateful for the gifted capacity to do so, that is, to make a positive difference for those who are listening.

I wonder how thinking about these questions has helped you to understand yourself better. Have your answers given you more confidence to entertain the notion of becoming a Musician Healer? I hope so.

TWELVE

PATIENS BALANCED HEALING

It occurs to me that this story is out of balance. So far, I've focused mainly on just one side of the healing equation—thc healer herself. This is ironic, since achieving balance is such an important aim of healing; truly the only way something can be whole.

The other day, a good friend and I were talking about hospice work, and how he had sung in a hospice choir at the deathbed. The idea that he and his singer friends were bringing a kind of healing to people in need was actually a new one for him. An interesting conversation ensued, when he asked me if I called the folks I work with 'patients'. I thought before I spoke, and said that I much preferred to call folks in need, 'people'. I dislike the term clients as well. Both terms are so removed, it feels, from the real flesh and blood, and heart and soul, of one who is in need of our help.

As these little experiences of inspiration go, the Latin word *Patiens* bubbled up in my mind. I spoke it out loud. My friend and I are both lovers of words, and word origins. So, it's not surprising that this reference to my years of Latin study, so many years ago, was ignited by the energy we were passing between us. He asked me the meaning, and I could only give him an incomplete definition, but one that I sensed was just right. "It has to do with affect, with disposition, an attitude of being." I began to realize that *patiens* and patient might actually be word clues to a human state that might beautifully describe some of those whom I work with. And the people on the other side of the healing equation must not be left out of this wondrous balance, most definitely.

Energy is a palpable force.
The healer and recipient person are
both active in cultivating,
setting up, and manipulating energies.

As soon as I returned home from our delightful brunch and conversation, I ran to my old Latin/English dictionary, bought so many years ago, probably at a yard sale. This tome, almost four-inches thick, was published in 1866, the 27th Edition. Referred to so many times over the years, when I hold such an old book in my hands, it often feels like important clues are about to be given, and I'd better pay close attention. So I do.

Here's the definition I found: *Patiens:* suffering, bearing; allowing, permitting; of a certain disposition.

So, I was right in saying that it is an attitude of being. It's obvious that someone who is ill or dying is very likely suffering and bearing difficulty. In fact, whether ill or dying or not, we are all bearing the burden, simply of being alive. But it's the 'allowing and permitting' that intrigues me the most. Indeed, allowing and permitting do have a great deal to do with successful outcomes when I share healing energies with people.

Successful healing is a cooperative venture. The energies I have to share will lose their strength if they run into resistance. These energies seek out an open and willing receptacle, in the form of a person who believes and trusts and relaxes into receivership. One who feels worthy and deserving of help. When these channels are open, we can work together to affect positive change. When they are closed, or only partially open, the results are less effective. I have said before in this book that I do not work alone. I rely on my spirit helpers to work with me, yes, but I also rely on my patients to work with me as well. This is teamwork of the highest order.

Energy is a palpable force. The healer and recipient person are both active in cultivating, setting up, and manipulating energies. You have read in the previous chapters how I do this. But the setting up of a deep receptacle within oneself as a recipient person is also very important in this process. As healer, I work with a creative force, an outwardly directed energy, channeled through me by powerful sources. It is very much yang energy. It is a benevolent force which moves through me. We have seen how I prepare myself to be able to do this. The recipient, too, must prepare himself to be a receptacle of this energy. This is yin. Receptivity is not a passive state, be cautioned. It is an active preparation of the mind and body, which involves intentional quieting, emptying, trusting, and opening. And perhaps most important, believing that he or she is worthy of help and health.

This is a tall order. Living in the world has taught us all that personal protection and boundaries are necessary for survival. In too many cases, it has also taught us that we are less-than-wondrous beings, that we do not deserve the best, that our flaws and failings as human beings make us unworthy. Perhaps we were told this in one fashion or another as children. Or as students in school. Or while in abusive relationships of any kind.

These judgmental pronouncements have a way of making very comfortable homes within our minds and can remain there throughout our lives. Taking on the hard work of healing ourselves throughout adulthood can begin to clean up this awful mess. But it's absolutely necessary if we wish to make ourselves receptacles to every good thing in life. We need to learn to love ourselves again. To ask for help when needed, without shame. To receive loving care with joy and gratitude.

Imagery that my sister uses in her prayer life perfectly describes this cooperative process of giving and receiving. She sees herself holding a large jar of golden honey and tipping it to pour its goodness into a deep empty bowl. The concave vessel opens itself to all that is given, until it is gradually filled with its goodness. She imagines the bowl is the whole world, all its people, creatures, plants, waters, mountains, so that her healing prayer reaches all the Earth. Isn't this beautiful? Let me share two more stories that show how resistance and receptivity can affect healing outcomes.

Resistant Energy

I had been working with a dying man and his family during the final days of his life in a hospital hospice suite. He and his wife had welcomed my presence and were grateful for the peaceful energy that they felt as a result of the work. He was declining quickly, and I was finally called in one morning by a nurse who said he was actively dying. When I knocked on the door and let myself in, I saw that at least a dozen friends and family members surrounded his bed. I expected to be able to quietly join them, to breathe and sing, as I had done before. But surprise. One of the big burly brothers of the man turned to look at me as I entered, gave me a glaring warning while rising from his seat, and vigorously approached me. I took a step back, feeling the power of his energy, sensing anger and hostility.

I attempted to explain who I was, and why I was there, but he wouldn't have any of it. He said: "Get out!" This fellow was, obvious to me, full of fear and perhaps the shameful feeling (for a man) of helplessness, in the face of his brother dying—all of which translated to anger and a nearly violent escort out the door. I decided to retreat, while catching the apologetic eye of the bereaved wife, who looked as though she wished I could have been able to break through the resistance. But there was nothing to be done. The resistant energy of the brother was just too much force to counter, and I chose not to bring any more confusion or distress into the room. Definitely something that the dying man did not need.

Even though the resistant force was not housed within the patient himself, it successfully prevented me from being able to pour any honey into his vessel. After recovering from my fright, I was left feeling sad and sorry. It's interesting to note that a nurse had sensed something amiss, so strong was the energy being pressure cooked in the room. Thankfully, the nurse literally caught me in the hallway as I exited, followed by the angry brother, and the nurse used his calmer, stronger energy to deescalate the event.

Little Eagle

In contrast, I'd like you to meet my friend Little Eagle, whose ability to open and receive surpasses many I have worked with. He is a small, but rugged man—a carpenter by trade who has demanded a lot of his body over the years. He is 75 years old and was recently diagnosed with lung cancer. As fortune would have it, we met in an unusual but fortuitous way. Driving home from work one day, he spied the barn quilt depicting an eagle on a high branch which decorates my front porch. The next time he drove by, he pulled in and knocked on my door. When he learned that my name is Runningdeer, he told me he was Blackfoot and Irish, another person of Indigenous heritage, like myself. And, he told me that he was a healer. "Would you like to come to a fire ceremony I'm having next weekend by the water?" I recognized the opening of another door immediately and accepted his kind and friendly invitation.

Little Eagle eventually recognized me as another healer. I hadn't told him. But he knew. When cancer was discovered in his chest, he asked if I would bring him healing. He said: "I'm a healer. But I can't heal myself. I don't know why. But I can't." So, of course, I agreed. For several months now I've visited him at intervals, bringing along my basket of tuning forks. Little Eagle didn't know about tuning forks but understood me when I explained that sound and music were the tools I work with. He works with fire, sage, crystals, eagle feathers, and his hands. He has touched me, and his calloused hands are full of energy, warm and steady. Each of our ways is backed by compassion, prayer, calling upon spiritual help, strong intention and focused energy. So, we share much common ground.

Little Eagle is *patiens* in the truest sense. He suffers and bears his physical pain. He is one of those men who works physically hard and pays for it at the end of the day. And now that cancer has moved in, he bears the pain of that as well. But when I come to apply sound frequencies to his body and mind, he opens up like a flower. He breathes deeply, allows his body to relax, often prays aloud to the ancestors: "*sitsanoma ambedeka,*" (my phonetic spelling of what I hear), calling on them to be present while we share this holy time. We work together, in concert, all of us, he and I and those unseen.

His oncologist and surgeon tell him that the cancer's growth has been arrested. He is pleased. His doctor knows about the healing work we are doing together, and as foreign as it may seem to him, he says: "Keep it up. It's working." So we will.

It's working because Little Eagle believes in the power. It's working because I believe in the power. It's working because cancer is an organic manifestation of chaotic vibrational energies within the body, so often resulting from past life trauma. (I happen to know that Little Eagle's childhood was full of abuse, so there you have it.) Application of pure tones via tuning forks helps to reorganize those inner vibrations, helping to create order where there has been disorder. Healing ensues. I also believe that, because of the degradation that he has suffered in his life, his sense of worthiness has been wounded. And perhaps that's why he cannot apply his healing power to himself. He needed me to help channel those merciful and comforting energies into his being, and to teach him that he deserves to be well taken care of. I am honored to do be able to do that.

Little Eagle and I complete the healing circle. I direct the Creative Force, he receives it. The healing equation is balanced. I always leave his house on the tidal creek satisfied and inspired. Often with a jar of homemade CBD salve or a mason jar full of Three Sisters soup, traded in barter for my service. Ho!

THIRTEEN

REMARKABLE EFFECTS

As remarkable as the effects of music and sound are with those who are dying, our music can light up the lives of those who are still living and who may continue to live for quite a while, in the dark world of dementia and other elder diseases.

Every week I pack up my music bag with a diverse menu of piano and vocal music and walk into nursing home and memory care facilities scattered throughout northern and central Vermont. These are the places where our Elders—those too difficult to care for at home, and sadly, sometimes those who are no longer wanted because of the inconvenience they bring to their younger relatives—are brought to live out the rest of their days. Such is our modern culture, that many old folks are segregated from normal daily life, for the sake of keeping things more manageable for working families. Despite the good care they receive at the particular places where I am lucky to work, I see a lot of sadness, fear, agitation, anger, and remoteness. As well, I see, among them, courage, fortitude, and a determination to make the best of things.

I often think that the ones in deepest dementia are

the more fortunate, since they live within their own psychic worlds where who knows what is going on? Maybe it's something better. But often not. The big question I face each time I walk into these so-called 'homes away from homes' is: How can my music help? How can I make this better for everyone?

This was answered for me one day by a woman named Dora who had been a resident for nearly four years. She was an accomplished artist, a person who had lived a lively intellectual life with enriching relationships and experiences. At this point in her long journey, nearing her 100th birthday, she was burdened by advancing dementia and the general breakdowns of old age. She had been a faithful attendee at our weekly music groups, always taking a seat as close to the piano as possible. Being a long-time observer of all things visible, and still having sufficient mental capacity to communicate about what she saw, she reported to me:

> I am amazed at what happens when you come. When you play this beautiful music, everything here in this room changes. So many of these people wake up! When this isn't happening, most of them are lost or sleeping. It's hard to believe the change.

This is what happens when our aim is to bring attention to the moment through our senses.

I learned the importance of changes brought about by music when I first read about the Zen Hospice Project in its early days as a small residential hospice facility in San Francisco. This was forty years ago, and the wisdom of their approach made perfect sense to me. These days, mindfulness practice is finally reaching far and wide. But there is no better place for it than while working with people who have nearly 'lost their minds' to dementias. For people who can no longer easily access their past memories, nor project and plan for their futures, the moment is what they have, their most accessible entree into living. So, I do what I can to bring them here, into the right now.

What I notice in these settings is almost immediate when I walk into the room, where up to twenty or more people in wheelchairs gather around the piano, patiently awaiting my arrival. Many of us have built long-time relationships, so I am easily recognizable. Those who are more cognitive and awake smile and greet me with enthusiasm. "We've been waiting for this all week," some will announce. As I go around the room with greetings, those who are less verbal and more remote are beginning to stir a bit, and when the first sounds from the piano ring out, small signs of life gradually appear. Those 'walkers', who are not wheelchair bound, especially those with Alzheimer's who like to walk out their energy, often shuffle towards the piano, curious and more engaged. One or two in wheelchairs will move themselves so close to the instrument that staff have to pull them away a bit so I have enough room to play. They are wakened and drawn in by the music and the energy I am transmitting through it.

As the hour passes, sometimes the most remote among them will sing, remembering words to old songs from their long ago past. One or two may dance. Others will express emotion through tears, laughter, or looks of longing, as they feel more connected to the moment which bears many emotions, memories, colors, physical sensations; all those human qualities that music has a unique way of representing, expressing, and drawing out. Those who need to sleep will be comforted by the gentle pieces I play or sing. In fact, those who were most energetic at my arrival are often napping deeply at the end of our time together.

As long as I am in good shape energetically myself,
have carefully pulled together a program that will
resonate with the needs of my listeners,
and intend the greater good for all involved,
good results come to pass.

I mustn't forget the response of staff. Many wander into the big room to have a taste of music and energetic refreshment before moving on to their duties. One man in particular, who works in the adjoining kitchen, always makes a point of doing his kitchen duty during the music hour. He voices his enjoyment very simply: "This is so good!" I suspect he's feeling the goodness for himself but is also recognizing the great goodness it is for all these people in his care.

The amazing thing is that these kinds of results in group work are consistent with every visit I make. No exceptions. As long as I am in good shape energetically myself, have carefully pulled together a program that will resonate with the needs of my listeners, and intend the greater good for all involved, it comes to pass.

To elaborate, let me zoom in again on Dora to add more detail to the picture. Just one person among the many, her individual response to musical experience, over a period of four years of weekly exposure, right up until her death, reveals many rich personal features that tell a fuller story.

Dora's Story

Encountering Dora at the nursing home, again after many years, was a surprise. We had met twenty years earlier, at a meeting of women doing peace and justice work in Vermont. She had recently published a book about remarkable women in the state and the work that they did, so I was casily drawn to this beautiful Elder who was then in her late 70s. I visited her at her nearby home and art studio, read the book, and loved her even more. Our personal contact ended there, as each of us became caught up in our lives. That is until I instantly recognized her one day after arriving for my group session at the nursing home, where she had just been admitted.

When I approached her, I wondered if she would recognize and remember me. She did not. It was as if we were meeting for the first time. She was 96 years old, was clearly in the mid-stage of dementia (possibly Alzheimer's, though I never felt the need to have that particular information). I invited her to sit in on our music group, just about to start, and she was more than willing. As a new resident, she was disoriented and in need of special attention, so I invited her to sit in a chair right next to the piano, so close that she could watch my every move at the keyboard and I could keep a close watch over her. After one session of classical music, vintage dance music from the early days of her life, and a series of lovely songs, she was hooked. I had made a new, old friend.

From that day on, Dora was always present at our weekly session, unless ill and bedbound. As the months passed, our relationship grew, so eager was she to share and show what she was experiencing. Not completely wheelchair bound, she worked very hard to get to the gathering room with her walker. Ever the bohemian, I can see her in my mind's eye dressed in a long peasant skirt cinched with a broad belt around her ever shrinking waist, carefully backing herself into her special chair. With comradely humor, we called it 'her throne.' She continued to do this for four years, right through her 100th birthday, which we all, residents and staff, celebrated together with pizzazz. She was weakening more and more, her frail thin body not able to muster much energy. When I played the snappy foxtrots of the 1930s, her feet took over, moving with the jaunty beat, bringing back the kinesthetic memory of dancing with her artist husband in New York City, where they lived and worked on Bleeker Street for many years. The music helped her recall stories about meeting Billy Holiday, 'Lady Day' and inviting her to dinner at their apartment. Her memory, awakened by the musical sounds of the day, came alive for the hour and gave her energy to share some of the important times of her life. She often said, "My feet just can't stop moving. They love it! I love it!"

Some days she would be in a fog, confused, fearful of "losing my mind"—but able to tell me so. Not only with a few words but through her hunched posture and ashen face. Gentle, classical music would often draw out her tears. "You make me cry. The music makes me cry." I would always assure her that was a good thing. She needed to clean out her difficult emotions. She would not necessarily be the only one in the room with tears streaming. With many of these folks missing home, feeling lonely, confused, and anxious, crying in a supported environment was a much-needed relief.

Often, on better days while in a more lucid state, Dora's intellect would kick in, and she'd ask about composers, the era the music was written in, and such. A few others became interested as well, creating openings for me to relate to those few with more cognitive faculties intact.

Without fail, at the end of each hour, Dora would say: "Is it really over? Has an hour gone by? Must you leave?" So captivated by the music was she (and others I might add), her sense of time was altered. It felt as if time both stood still and flew by with great speed. How does this happen? I believe that listening to beautiful music, infused with healing energy, is a holistic experience—an experience in which all our senses and faculties are stimulated and in balance with one another, where we are somehow delivered to another dimension and time as we know it does not exist. To be dosed with this kind of energy at least once a week is a special kind of medicine which every Elder in our care truly needs. Dora so often said, as I mentioned before, "Everything changes here when you come and play. It affects all of us. It's remarkable. I want you to know this."

And always, from not only Dora, but many, "When will you come back? Please come back soon."

I always reassure them, "Of course, I will be back next week. I love this too!"

My music followed Dora to her deathbed, at her venerable age of 100 years and several months. Hers was not the most peaceful death I would have wished for her. Nor were the four years she spent in the nursing home. Agitation, sadness, home sickness, and discouragement were her more-than-occasional visitors. As I sat and sang at her bedside, small indicators of relaxation would appear, small morsels when she could have used a five-course meal of it. Her paintings and drawings, hung on the walls, the colorful decor, the interesting placement of her bed which spoke of her individual taste and flair, the rows of books and art supplies that framed her small desk, all spoke to me of this wonderful, intelligent, creative woman who would leave her legacy of art, writing, activism, and friendship behind.

I am very grateful for having been reunited with this fine lady, and for being able to accompany her, with music, through the long final stage of her long, long life. One of my colleagues said it well: "For Dora, music was a light in a dark tunnel." Without her knowing, her story can now illustrate to my musician readers the good practice of administering music medicine to the oldest among us.

FOURTEEN

FROM ART TO MEDICINE WHAT TO PLAY?

We serious musicians have repertoires. Our repertoires obviously include music that we love to play. Our repertoires grow over the years, and now that I am 73 years old, and having made music since I was a small child, my repertoire is quite large. It has grown with me. It reflects my wide taste in genres and styles, some of it based on many years of classical music study, some of it based on vintage music and jazz I heard while growing up, some of it based on years of choral singing, some of it drawn from folk and traditional music I have loved listening to since I was a teen and young adult. My great love of music has opened doors to all sorts of musical expression. The music I have loved best, I have learned either to play on the piano, or to sing. I bring a vast library of music to my work, and from that I can choose what is appropriate for any group or individual I might be working with.

In addition to all these musical works, there is the music that my listeners have loved. That music may or may not match the music that I know and love. Offering them our mutually beloved music is easy. But offering the music that I have not particularly been drawn to, or at times really dislike, presents a challenge that I have met in a creative way (which then makes it interesting and more likable to me).

The first rule of thumb about what to play is: play the music that you love. Period. And if someone requests something you don't love, make it lovable. How have I done this? I recall a man in my care who was a great Hank Williams fan. Country music doesn't light me up, but it did him, so I took the old country classic, "I'm So Lonesome I Could Cry" and made it my own. The chord structure is simple, E flat, E flat7, A flat, E flat, E flat, B flat, E flat. The familiar lyrics about whippoorwills, midnight trains whining low, and losing the will to live are so poignant and meaningful to people that once I settled into this song, I grew to love them too.

For the fellow who was dying and loved this plaintive song, I played a spare arrangement at my digital keyboard, using the dreamy electric piano font (the one that sounds like an old Fender Rhodes), and sang the verses very slowly. Mournfully. It was exquisite, and we both loved it, with tears streaming. This man, now long dead, gave me this song as his parting gift. It will forever be in my repertoire of favorites.

The older I get, the more I encounter people of my own generation and age, either in nursing homes or in their deathbeds at hospital. We all grew up in the forties, fifties, and sixties, when rock 'n' roll fired us up through adolescence, young adulthood, and beyond. I still love much of the classic rock of those days, but to play such raucous music in healthcare facilities isn't often appropriate, or even helpful healthwise. But I've had patients request slow, thoughtful songs by Black Sabbath, Lynyrd Skynrd, The Band, and others that have come to life in a new way, through my voice and the use of simple percussion instruments. "After Forever," "Freebird," and "I Shall be Released," each shared with my own vocal interpretation, accompanied by a Native American medicine drum or shruti box or simple shakers, brought something meaningful and familiar to my contemporaries at a time when the very personal touched deep places.

A Universal Language

Music is a universal language with many dialects. As musicians, we have the skills and artistry available to stretch, to be more inclusive in our musical choices. We are meant to serve our listeners, after all. But the gift should always be in our own voices and decorated by our own musical sensibilities. Think of doing your own 'cover' of a popular song and make it your own.

I love to sing songs in the languages of each family's national heritage. It has helped tremendously that, as a voice major in conservatory, I studied French, Italian, Spanish, Latin, and German. I recently sang at the bedside of a man who was Croatian and found a lullaby in his native language (he was an immigrant who had not mastered English). I needed to consult his son about the pronunciations, which included the son in an important process. This song was medicine for a family that carried lots of anxiety during a long death vigil.

The vast treasury of classical piano music is a mainstay for me—my most beloved music. The sonatas of Schubert, Mozart, Haydn, Beethoven, Scarlatti are so often included. The tempi and moods of various movements are so differentiated that I can select particular ones to suit a particular need: to calm, to energize, to elevate, to dream. Even those listeners who have never been exposed to the classics are affected by its beauty and learn to love something new in the late stage of life. I have often told the story of how my siblings and I fell asleep to our mother's playing of Debussy and Chopin, when we were children. Now, as Elders, they get to enjoy something like that.

My Musical Selections

I'm about to pack my bag with music for a group session I'll play tomorrow at a facility for people with various stages of advancing dementia. Let's see what I put in...

Handel, *Suite No. 9 for Harpsichord* (played on piano). Three movements, but played in more moderate *tempi*

Haydn, *Sonata no. 17 in B-flat Major*. Two movements, *Allegro* and *Andante*

Four Ancient French Christmas Carols (sung, with piano)

George Winston's arrangement of *Carol of the Bells*

Debussy, *Arabesque No. 1*

Collection of vintage popular songs from 1920s, '30s, '40s, '70s (sung, with piano)

Irving Berlin, "Always," 1925 (sung, with piano)

Roy Turk, "Walkin' My Baby Back Home," 1930 (sung, with piano)

Sammy Fain, "I'll Be Seeing You," 1938 (sung, with piano)

Jule Styne, "Let It Snow," 1945 (sung, with piano)

Stephen Sondheim, "Send in the Clowns, from A Little Night Music," 1973 (sung, with piano)

Mozart, *Andante* movement from *Sonata, K. 545*

Meredith Wilson, "May the Good Lord Bless and Keep You," 1950 (sung, with piano)

Let's look at the reasons for choosing this music. Firstly, I do love it all. It's in my hands and voice. Although I could change my mind at the last minute and choose another movement from Haydn or Mozart which is less familiar to me. Sight reading comes easily to me, and that particular musical activity lights up additional areas of my brain which enhance the energy transmission I'm sharing with listeners. It also keeps me on my toes and brings something new and fresh to the repertoire. It's a week before Christmas, and it's an opportunity to share unfamiliar music of the season. The ancient French carols are favorites of mine, and a nice break from the more familiar songs people are inundated with this time of year, even in nursing homes.

I open the hour with Handel, lovely delicate music played in a moderate tempo (even though its markings are allegro), which will gently wake my listeners up and establish an easy body rhythm. Handel is followed by Haydn, which is sunny in mood and buoyant in spirit. After the French carols, I return to the graceful piano music of Debussy's *Arabesque*, an opportunity to dream.

As long as I am in good shape energetically myself,
have carefully pulled together a program that will
resonate with the needs of my listeners,
and intend the greater good for all involved,
good results come to pass.

The set of vintage songs which follows is designed to move alternately from slow and thoughtful to lively and stimulating in a couple of cycles. These are the songs of my listeners' youth (these people were all born in the 1920s and 30s), and dementia will not stop them from remembering lyrics, singing along, and dancing in their wheelchairs. Memories may be evoked from these long-ago times, and it's not unusual for someone to talk about that vibrant part of their life.

I close the session by winding down the energy level

with a Mozart Andante movement from the many piano sonatas I love. And then sing some of these folks to sleep again with a sweet song of blessing. I expect the room will be quiet, under a spell, when I finish (it so often is). I'll stand and look at all of them, some faces beaming, others asleep, several voicing their thanks and love of it all. I walk about, take their hands, touch their heads, and let them know how fine it is for me to share this time with them, because it most certainly is. I feel both calm and energized, very nicely put together. Music played and shared in this loving and intentional way rewards me, as its instrument of delivery, as much as it does my listeners. We are all blessed.

How would you build an hour-long program for a group of people who need some tender, loving care? First, think about the intended effects you'd like the music to have on your listeners. Then consider the flow of those effects: gently arousing, sustained alertness, calming, sleep-inducing, dancing, memory evoking, inspiring, spiritual, mood elevating, imaginative. Each of these can be ordered appropriately, depending on the perceived needs of your listeners. Look at your own repertoire and make selections based on how that music affects you personally. Your human response to music is not unlike that of your listeners, after all.

A Little Touring Journey

I think of each session as a little touring journey, with brief stop-offs at various internal places of sensual/mental/emotional experience. I'm the tour guide, and we get to enjoy this little trip together. The people I play for are generally confined to small worlds within facilities. They long for expansion of experience, a change in routine, something new and gently stimulating. A vacation from the challenges of illness and senility. We musicians can bring a freshness and rejuvenation to their lives that can stay with them for days after the actual journey. A vividness that nourishes the human spirit and gives them something to look forward to.

One of the most frequent pieces of feedback I get from staff and patients and residents alike is: "We've been waiting for you to come. We're so happy you are here. How soon will you come back?" This kind of engagement with life is the food that we all crave, young and old, sick or well. The medicine of music can help us all truly live, until we die.

FIFTEEN

CROSSING THE GREAT WATER

"For only the man who goes to meet his fate resolutely is equipped to deal with it adequately. Then he will be able to cross the great water—that is to say, he will be capable of making the necessary decision and of surmounting the danger."

—I Ching, Taoist Book of Changes and Oracles
Hexagram #5, Hsu

ACCOMPANYING ONE who is dying with beautiful music is a unique privilege and experience, unlike any other. It has taken a lifetime, long or short, for a person to reach this place of dying. Living, for them, has been a piece of work. But the final approach to actual death or end of life is such a powerful and awesome piece of work—not unlike the original journey down the birth canal—that special tribute and understanding must be made. We musicians who accompany this process must offer a presence which is most sensitive, centered, strong, and calm. There is much to learn as we offer our music and energy at the deathbed. With eyes, ears, and hearts open, we can enter the liminal space occupied by the one before us, as she Crosses the Great Water, to experience some of the mysteries that reside there.

The I Ching

I have consulted the I Ching for most of my adult life. The Taoist tradition has a very sensible and holistic way of understanding the constant change through which we must all maneuver during a lifetime. The virtues it has helped me to develop—patience, keen observance, finding satisfaction in small progress, humility and assertiveness both, acting at the opportune time, keeping still in non-action—all these skills have helped me to find an easier flow in my life of twists and turns. Easy flow is where we experience peace and productivity, competence and progress, trust, and courage. This kind of flow is no less important in dying than it is in living. In fact, it may be most important at this stage, the ultimate piece of work which is ours to do on this plane.

Crossing the Great Water is an image which reappears numerous times in the I Ching. It represents taking on a big challenge. I see the Great Water as a very wide river, riddled with currents, obstacles, dangers. To cross it requires time, effort, energy, courage, and commitment. We are called to cross many such rivers in our lifetimes, but the final crossing over to death, a destination of great mystery, can be the most perilous. The Book of Changes gives good counsel about how to face and surmount these dangers, so again, it is well worth listening to the ancient sages when planning and executing this grand crossing.

While working with the dying, I have witnessed many go through a period of ambivalence about living or dying. You might think that we have little choice in the matter, but what we set our sights on truly matters in the end. Even those people who are quite aware of a terminal prognosis, even of short term, decide to cling to life as long as possible, and sometimes longer than is in their best interest. Clutching onto survival in a form that is familiar, even if the body is in stress and serious discomfort, is understandable. No judgment, another frequent phrase in the I Ching, by the way. But for all, there comes a time when the effort of staying alive becomes too much to bear, and a turning point arrives when the prospect of death, that unknown shore on the far side of the river, comes into clearer view. So then, how to proceed? We must decide to step into the Great Water.

Two contrasting stories from my own experiences with the dying shed some light on how important it is to make such a decision to move forward, into the water. My mother had been living with renal failure and other difficult conditions affecting her heart and lungs for seven years, through her late seventies and eighties. She was determined to stay alive, to be with her beloved family, by undergoing dialysis several times a week during those years. She lived a happy existence at home with family: cooking, playing the piano, listening to music, and being part of family events. The price she had to pay for this extended time with us, many hours each week in a local dialysis clinic, was one she was willing to take on. She did it well, in good spirits, even doing what she could to support others like her at the clinic who were having a more difficult time. She had been a nurse for decades, took a writing course at the end of her life, and proudly published a magazine article about incorporating dialysis into one's life with a positive attitude. She was a dear and remarkable woman.

As she entered this new and final phase,
I noticed spheres of light dancing on the wall,
connected to her body by a
long strand of thin light.

But, as sad as she was to leave us, she knew when it was time to give up the struggle to stay alive. At her advanced age, dialysis was no longer effective enough to keep her going; she was losing weight rapidly and had little energy. She knew her end days were near. So, she made her decision to die, to bow with grace to the natural forces that had authority.

One week before her sudden death from a quick heart attack, she called her sister-in-law, a close confidante, to tell her that she was letting go of her will to live, that she was ready, and to say goodbye. She didn't tell any of her children about this decision, her way of sparing us anguish. But she did talk with each of us during her week of preparation, very beautiful talks of love and how she hoped she would not be forgotten. We were all preparing quietly for her departure, though it would be a little sooner than we all might have guessed. During the week between her announcement to my aunt and her actual death, she paid all her personal bills, cleaned her little suite at my brother's home, put things in order, and sat down at her piano for the last time to play a beautiful song written long ago by my father for one of my sisters. She tried to sing as she played, although it was difficult. My brother duly noted this as a sign that she was doing important final things.

One week after this journey across the water began for my mother, she collapsed and immediately died while dressing one morning. She was spared the long death bed vigil, the abnormal breathing and death rattle congestion of a longer dying process, the extended time of continued diminishment that such a death involves. For that, I have been truly grateful. I am certain that her experience of pain and discomfort was very brief, if at all, and that her spirit zoomed out of her spent body with great speed and joy. But I am most grateful for the fact that she was clear in her mind about her approaching end of life, that she had decided to accept it and to commit herself to its activation. She stepped into the water, and with courage and determination, made it to the other side. It's one of those strange ironies that I never got to sing and play music for my own mother while she was dying.

In contrast, a few days ago I attended the dying of a man in his early seventies. He was in a hospice bed at the hospital where I work. He was struggling to breathe, still awake and alert, and full of fear. He would not close his eyes in fear of never opening them again. Already in the midst of Cheyne-Stokes breathing, rapid and shallow breaths followed by lengthening periods of apnea, he was in the long process of dying, which would actually go on for him another sixteen hours. His wife and adult daughter did their best to calm him down, but his fear was so deeply placed in his psyche and body that his struggle went on. I intervened and breathed with him, toning audibly on the outbreath, while his family looked on.

During his cyclic periods of apnea, I verbally encouraged him to simply float, to enjoy the rest. It took quite a while to convince this man to give it a try, but he did to a degree, and it gave him some temporary comfort. He managed a slight smile as I left an hour later, but I knew that his fear had not entirely been conquered. This man had not prepared, as my mother did, for death. He was fighting it, not bowing to its authority, and that's what made his struggle so difficult.

I sang a lovely song at the foot of his bed that morning. It's a river song titled "Love Call Me Home" by Peggy Seeger that includes words about how time ferries us down a river and how the love of friends calls us home. Such was this man's predicament. He needed friends and others to help him cross the river. He had a terrible time swimming on his own. We all did the best we could for him at this late stage. Sadly, but honestly, I would not call this a peaceful death.

Learning to Swim

I finally learned to swim, really swim, very late in life. When I was 65, I decided that it was time to start teaching my granddaughter to swim. When I was a child, a near drowning accident left me terrified of the water, and from then on, I stayed far from the shoreline, only able to observe all the fun my friends were having in the water. My resistance to learning how to swim was steadfast, just like my fearful dying patient. And I suffered through that, just as he did.

But something surprising happened when I was a senior in undergraduate college. In order to qualify for receiving my degree, I was required to take a swimming test. Oh, no! Not obtaining my degree because of this possible deficit was simply out of the question. So, circumstances forced me to face the music. I nervously signed up for Swimming 101 and discovered on the first day of class, petrified as I was, that the pool was packed with others like myself who had never learned to swim. I managed to pass the simple swimming test at the end of the semester. I was not a great swimmer, but I knew how to stay afloat in deep water and managed to pull off a few basic strokes, which for me was a great achievement. I graduated with high honors. Sigh of relief.

I had at least overcome my greatest fear of setting foot in the water. But I can't say that for the next several decades I truly enjoyed swimming. That was to come much later, with the arrival of a granddaughter, and my wish to spare her the agonies I had endured around water. We began slowly, with the help of swimming lessons for the young, and then worked together to practice floating, putting our heads under water, holding our breath, dog paddling, and then, alas, swimming underwater.

As she learned, I learned. As she grew and became stronger in the water, I followed suit. When she finally passed her swim test at the local pool and jumped into ten feet of water, I cheered and clapped for both of us. It has been a few years since that happened, and now we swim together as often as we can. We create water ballet moves, use goggles, and swim underwater like mermaids. I can now swim long laps, controlling my easy breathing, feeling the strength and fluidity of my

As long as I am in good shape energetically myself,
have carefully pulled together a program that will
resonate with the needs of my listeners,
and intend the greater good for all involved,
good results come to pass.

body. And the wonderful ease with which I can now do these things. Without fear. Without fear. Without fear.

When I float on my back, I consciously think about what it will be like to float during the apnea of my own death. I keep practicing that blessed feeling of letting my body go, allowing the water to hold me up, like the arms of a strong mother. Never would I have expected to be able to do this at this late stage of life. But my decision, my commitment, my courage, and practice have led me to this glorious achievement. My granddaughter, a little Pisces, is a natural and happy swimmer who says, "Meme, the water is my world!" As it is now mine. I think we may both be well prepared whenever it is that each of us will die.

Just as learning to really, really swim has taken me more than seventy long years to fully develop, I think that preparing to die, to cross that great water, is also a lifelong course of study. If we don't start early to think about this passage, to allow ourselves some of the emotions, including fear, that taking this on evokes, to learn the important skills of relaxation, to practice the art of flow in our active lives, we won't be ready for the final swim. And it will undoubtedly be very hard. We can avoid drowning in those waters if we talk about death, be present for those in our lives who are dying, being honest with ourselves and others about the natural course of things. In our death-phobic culture, this often still feels like going against the grain. Modern medicine and the quest for longer lives has not only led to some benefits but unfortunately reinforced an aversion to death that does not serve any of us well. I encourage you to get in the water, trust its strength, explore its joys. Swim.

Spiritual Waters

I'll end my thoughts on death, floating, swimming, and preparing for crossing the great water, with a list of river songs I often sing at the death bed. Black American slaves bequeathed us a rich collection of spirituals, many of which beautify, with music, the crossing of deep waters, deep rivers. My favorite is "Deep River," a Black spiritual song that was first mentioned in print in 1867:

Sheet music for Henry T. Burleigh's 1917 arrangement of "Deep River"
Author of the song, unknown.
(Historic American Sheet Music collection at Duke University)

Deep River
My home is over Jordan
Deep River
I want to cross over into campground

Another is “Stan’ Still Jordan,” (predating 1860):

Stan’ still Jordan
Stan’ still Jordan
Stan’ still Jordan
Lord, I can’t stand still

I got a mother in heaven
I got a mother in heaven
I got a mother in heaven
Lord, I can’t stand still

Jordan River
Jordan River
Jordan River is chilly and cold

A gorgeous, prayerful song called “Keep Me from Sinkin’ Down” is a direct plea for help while swimming... (predating 1860):

Oh Lord, Oh my good Lord
Keep me from sinkin’ down
Oh Lord, Oh my good Lord,
Keep me from sinkin’ down

I tell you what I mean to do;
Keep me from sinkin’ down
I mean to go to heav’n too,
Keep me from sinkin’ down

Look up yonder and what do I see;
Keep me from sinkin' down
I see the angels beckonin' me
Keep me from sinkin' down

Oh Lord, Oh my good Lord
Keep me from sinkin' down

A more lively plantation song was "Oh Wasn't Dat a Wide River?" (predating 1860):

O wasn't dat a wide river
dat river of Jordan, Lord
Wide river!
Dere's one mo' river to cross
Oh the river of Jordan is so wide
One mo' river to cross
I don't know how to get on de other side
One mo' river to cross

Wasn't dat a wide river
dat river of Jordan, Lord
Wide river!
Dere's one mo' river to cross

Beyond the simple yet meaningful words, the melodies and harmonies of these wondrous songs are gorgeous and heartfelt. So perfect at the bedside.

The later-dated American folk song tradition features many river songs as well. "The Water is Wide," "Michael Row the Boat Ashore," "Down to the River to Pray," to name a few.

I've also sung "Ol' Man River," "Cry Me a River," the old Christian hymn "On Jordan's Stormy Banks I Stand," and "Swimming to the Other Side" at the deathbed.

You must do your own search of river songs, ones that you love to sing or play, to make your own list. You will find that every musical genre, every cultural tradition, every language has embraced the theme of Crossing the Great Water. We all, every one of us on this Earth, will someday die, as so many have gone before us. The challenge of this crossing has been a part of life forever, so of course people have made songs with this universal theme and sung them forever. It is a rich musical treasury. If you are a musician who will grace the deathbed with your music, learn these songs and use them to help the dying swim to the other side.

FIFTEEN

JUST REWARDS

WALKING INTO THIS WORK, at midlife, literally saved my life. Approaching 50, I had already made and taught music in various venues but my inner world was troubled. Something was breaking out of me that was experiencing a very difficult birth. For seven years, during my forties, the birthing pains manifested as psychosomatic pain, deep depression, anxiety, and despair. I was in the world, but my place in it had not been fully established. What was my real work? And would I ever be well again?

When the door opened to making music in service to others and especially those who were suffering, my own deep healing began. It took some years for me to fully recover. Deep healing always takes time. But the more I opened to the idea that my music could likewise open others to an experience of healing, large or small, the more I healed. While offering music to the dying, I was learning how to trust the innate powerful potential of music. But most importantly, I was learning how to trust myself and my own personal power to affect healing in others. That is not a small thing. Over time, I settled into this ability. I am now at ease when I offer my music and my energy to others. I have learned to expect positive outcomes; therefore, the more they appear.

Our Own Healing and Evolution

Healing with music is a circular process. It is not a one-way street. I do not have magic powers to fix others. But I do know how to heal myself by inhabiting music as I play. When I feel that healing working on me, I can trust that it's working on others in my energy field. We enjoy healing together. Our energies become synchronized.

However, there are days when I'm tired, distracted, and my ability to create the healing circle of power is weakened. I am a mere human being, after all, affected by the stressors of my life. If I'm not feeling that "all put together" sensation while I'm playing, then I can be certain that my listeners are not receiving the best benefit that is possible. Then I must return to the work of calming and centering myself again. By and large, though, because I take good care of myself [6], these weaker sessions are few and far between.

The longer I do this work, the more deeply healed, in the sense of experiencing sustained wholeness, I have become. I'm not boastful. This doesn't make me someone special. It's simply the result of continually being exposed to a generative healing power that this work creates. And all that good stuff just gets recycled back into the music I make, in service to others. Everybody wins. I couldn't think of a more satisfying way to spend my work life.

[6] A complete chapter on Self-Care is included in my first book, *Musical Encounters with Dying: Stories and Lessons*, Jessica Kingsley Publishers. (2013)

There are a few very particular aspects of healing for myself that I've enjoyed these past twenty-plus years while developing my work as Musician Healer. Yours will be different, perhaps, depending upon what your own inner challenges to growth have been. Our stories are different, after all. For me, I finally found a true calling. A kind of work that really fits.

Because I've been successful, I now have a more solid and unique place in the world. I'd never felt that before in my life. I now know who I am, and why I'm here. I love and accept all my strengths, peculiarities, and tender places. And feel great confidence in what I have to offer the world.

As an artist, I usually have an abundance of creative energy. This work gives me a regular outlet for that energy, keeping a flow moving that is so beneficial to health. When creativity is blocked, especially in artistic people, illness often ensues. My seven desperate years of illness and real agony resulted, I believe in part, from a long-time blockage of creative energy in my life. Now that I play music at least four or five times each week, in different settings, my creative energy finds an easy and frequent channel of expression, and I remain well.

Sharing what I do well with many people gives me the great feeling of being seen, heard, and felt by many others. My unique talents are finally used, appreciated, and acknowledged. I feel needed and wanted. This is something else that is not a small thing. And the great surprise is I have not had to put myself into a prefabricated box to receive this. I've discovered my true self in a kind of work that supports my own design and have dared to offer that.

As a life-long introvert, I still maintain a quiet and private life that nourishes my nature. But this work enables me to be among many people in intimate ways. This way of relating to people is what I love. Over the years, I've grown a very large human family, where I've found a useful role and where I am warmly embraced. I feel like I belong. Toko-pa Turner writes: "May you feel shored up, supported, entwined, and reassured as you offer yourself and your gifts to the world."[7]

I do.

Show and Tell

As wonderful as my work life is, it is not without certain drawbacks and challenges. It took me years to figure out how to make sufficient money to support a modest lifestyle without burning out. You will undoubtedly find out that the world is slow to change, and until you can prove the value of your work over and over again, hospitals, nursing homes, hospices, and individuals may not yet recognize the monetary value of what you do. But please don't let that stop you. Dare, as I have, to show those who doubt that this kind of healing makes a positive and much-needed difference. Show and tell; show and tell. Over time, that can translate into making a living as a Musician Healer. That is just reward.

Then there's the matter of having to play a mediocre (if that) instrument. If you're a flutist, you won't have this problem. But as a pianist, I face this from time to time. I used to cart around a now-too-heavy (for me) digital piano, but I no longer am able to do that without strain. And besides, I much prefer playing an acoustic piano. So, I rely on the instruments that are on site.

[7] Toko-pa Turner. *Belonging: Remembering Ourselves Home.* Her Own Room Press, (2017) Dedication page.

Insisting on regular tunings is important, of course. But I sometimes must play a piano that must be coaxed to really sing. Making the best of what I have to work with is a good exercise and challenge. It humbles me, yes, and it also strengthens my ability to be flexible and particularly sensitive to what an old, tired piano might need from me in order to find a pleasing voice. It keeps me on my toes and makes me appreciate all the more the better instruments that some facilities are able to provide.

If your work is good, and noticed, you may be able to promote the idea of an institution obtaining a worthy piano. Too many nursing homes, in particular, have pianos that someone donated perhaps just to get rid of it. These instruments were likely not well-cared for over many years of use or abuse. We shouldn't blame facility administrators for not knowing about what makes a good piano. They usually just don't know. But we musicians do know and can educate and promote improvements.

Taking Time

Another hazard to be mindful of... the uninterested, stale feeling that comes from playing the same pieces too often, for too long. Fortunately, my repertoire is large, and the styles of music I play vary. If you work a lot, you may not have much time to keep learning and adding new music to your repertoire. You must pay close attention if this staleness creeps in because it may affect your ability to deeply engage and create the energetic circle of healing. If you are bored, your listeners will experience that too. That is definitely not our aim.

Lately, I myself have noticed a staleness setting in, and I've made an effort to find new pieces to learn and love. Isaac Albeniz' *Sonata no. 3, Opus 68,* for piano is now on the music desk of my grand piano at home, and I'll be sinking my teeth into it as soon as I return home from a much-needed three-day retreat, during which I've been writing this chapter.

I've spent these days at a spiritual retreat center on the coast of Maine, run by an order of Catholic sisters who welcome people of all spiritual orientations. It has offered me an environment of silence and simplicity, the refreshing sounds and energy of the sea, and un-pressured time to finish writing this book. The deep and restful sleep I had last night, after being lulled by the rhythms of ocean surf floating through my wide-open window, has led to this perfect beach day of thinking and writing. Sitting by this wondrous, ever-moving great body of water, the thoughts and words have truly poured out of me. So happy am I, taking this time for myself and feeling the pulsing flow of creative energy cycling through me.

To do this important work well, you will have to take the best care of yourselves. The high quality of energy you cultivate within can then be given to others, delivered by the beautiful music you love to make.

Loving Yourself

Love yourselves as much as you love music. This is the deepest inner work that is required. To do this, to really feel that self-love may take your lifetime to achieve. But keep practicing. Allow yourself to rest when you need it, without guilt. Comfort yourself when you feel sad or lonely. Praise yourself when you have manifested something wonderful and helpful in the world. Make decisions that benefit you, even while some in your life may not understand. Ask for help when you need it, from whatever sources sustain you, human or spiritual.

Perhaps most importantly, forgive yourself. Forgive yourself for all the sins of commission or omission you most likely have committed in your lifetime. We are all flawed; it's a condition of living. And the only way we can heal from guilt and shame is to become humble, to accept weakness in ourselves and others, and then to grant pardon for our humanness. Work on this because it won't come easily, and then feel this compassionate love in a big way while you sing or play in service to others.

At the beginning of this book there is a quote by Rabindranath Tagore. We can complete the circle of our explorations with this reminder:

> I slept and dreamed that life was joy.
> I awoke and found that life is but service.
> I served and discovered that service was joy.

What could be a better just reward
than joy?

Let's serve the suffering world
with our music

and

bask in it.

POSTSCRIPT

A FINAL CEREMONY

THE INVITATIONS WENT OUT a few days ago, and the scene is set for a musical soirée and ceremony to honor my special guests: all the muses who have graced the pages of this book. The great hall is bare except for a grand piano at its center. Light streams in through its many tall windows. Flowers and candles adorn every corner. At the appointed hour of "no time," they begin to quietly float in and take a place in the circle surrounding the piano.

Nenet is first to arrive. How pretty she is, wearing the golden caduceus amulet on her left arm. She is followed by Pu-ra, Hetep and Ama. Behind them, Onatah, Donehogawa and Kajijonhawe, all decked in beaded skins and feathers. So peacefully they join the circle. A few moments later, little Jacquet, full of life and curiosity, escorted by his ever faithful companion Perpetuo, their simple, hooded cassocks an earthy toned contrast to the others' more colorful regalia. Claudin and Maud, in basic peasant garb, proud of their son's achievements, wouldn't miss this celebration for the world. Finally, Sri Ganapathi Sachidananda Swamiji, the only still-living guest arrives, adorned in peach and saffron. He is now too old to physically attend, so he has sent his etheric body to join us this evening, in 'no time'. The circle is now full, and I walk into its center, next to the piano, and bow in reverence and gratitude to them all.

Our communication is silent, deeply felt, and clear as a bell. I thank them for entering my world while writing the book, for sharing their stories with me, for giving me understanding and insight along the way. They tell me that I am doing good work, that it is my turn now to continue this music healing mission, and to pass along the teaching to others. I assure them that our book will do just exactly that. We are happy to be together, our hearts full and refreshed.

Without another thought, I sit at the piano and play for them. I quiet myself, breathe deeply, radiate the warm love I feel for each of them, and set my intention to fill their spirits with the purest mana of all Creation. With great thanks. I have chosen to play Alexander Borodin's *Intermezzo, No. 2* from his *Petite Suite for Piano.* It is a sweet and lyrical piece, graceful and flowing in minuet tempo. Midway, it briefly directs us into a more introspective spell, then releases us again into sunshine and spring. Remember Borodin and the researchers who brought music to their patients in early sound healing experiments? They must be here tonight, too, within the energy of this beautiful music.

As I play the final three F notes in the deep bass, each of my guests smiles and nods. Then one by one, they vanish into the ether. They depart as quietly as they came. I am left alone with my piano, and the future, in earthly time, that awaits me.

ACKNOWLEDGMENTS

DIFFERENT GROUPINGS of people have appeared throughout the various stages of my life, small cadres who've shown up to teach, to help move me forward, to encourage, and to share in the sorrows and joy.

This long period of writing *The Musician Healer* and preparing for its publication has been fielded by a small group of people who have crossed my path, some of whom have become very good friends—Judith Abbott, Olivia Hoblitzelle, for your deep probing feeling and thought; Lisa Jae, my dear sister and spiritual confidante; Lorene Shyba, publisher and editor at Durvile & UpRoute Books, who has carefully and sensitively midwifed this project; artists Mary Jo Fulmer and Rich Théroux, who put their imaginations to paint and paper, revealing the magic of this book. I would also like to sincerely thank Tanya Maggi, Mary Bonhag and Julian Hobson, for reading and understanding; for confirmation and confidence.

To Vicki Reeser, Mary and Rich Howe, and all those on my team at Deer Isle Sunset Congregational Church, on Deer Isle, Maine. You provided me with a wonderful, creative outlet during the past two years of pandemic. Your church gave me a place to share my art and my energy during such a strange and challenging time when we all needed to be uplifted by music.

BIBLIOGRAPHY

Amentet Neferet, “Hymns & Prayers, Ancient Egypt.” Facebook Page Amentet Neferet. Accessed December 15, 2015.

Betz, Hans Dieter, ed. (1986), *The Greek Magical Papyri in Translation.* Chicago. University of Chicago Press.

Budge, E.A. Wallis, Sir. (1995; originally published 1895), *The Book of the Dead.* New York, N.Y. Gramercy Books/ Random House.

Davison, James T.R., M.D. (October 28, 1899) “Music in Medicine”. *The Lancet, Journal of the American Medical Associatio*n, ii.

Elkaim, Yuri. “How to Do Belly-Breathing Like a Pro”. yurielkaim.com/belly-breathing/ Accessed October 2019.

Fenton, William N. (1942) “Songs from the Iroquois Longhouse: Program notes for an album of American Indian Music from the Eastern Woodlands.” Washington, D.C. Smithsonian Institute.

Fenton, William N. (2002) *The Little Water Medicine Society of the Senecas.* Norman, Oklahoma. University of Oklahoma Press.

Graves-Brown, Carolyn. (2010) *Dancing for Hathor: Women of Ancient Egypt.* A & C Black Publishers.

Haich, Elizabeth. (1965) *Initiation.* London. George Allen & Unwin Ltd.

Haimov-Kickman, Ronit et al. (2005) "Reproduction concepts and practices in ancient Egypt mirrored by modern medicine." *European Journal of Obstetrics and Gynecology and Reproductive Biology* 123, 3-8.

Keller, Cecilia. (2005) "Medicine in Matriarchal Societies." Second world Congress on Matriarchal Studies, Societies of Peace. Available at second-congress-matriarchal-studies.com/Keller.html. Accessed February 1, 2016.

Kemper, Kathy J., Shaltout, Hossam A., "Non-verbal communication of compassion: measuring psychophysiologic effects." BioMed Central Complementary and Alternative Medicine 2011 11:32, International Society for Complementary Medicine Research.

Kramer, Bruce & Wurzer, Cathy. (2015) *We Know How This Ends: Living While Dying.* University of Minnesota Press.

Mann, Barbara Alice. (2000) *Iroquoian Women: The Gantowisas.* New York, N.Y. Peter Lang.

Mark, J. J. (2017, February 21). Ancient Egyptian Medical Texts. World History Encyclopedia. Retrieved from https://www.worldhistory.org/article/1015/ancient-egyptian-medical-texts/

Meymandi, Assad, MD. (2009) "Music, Medicine, Healing and the Genome Project." *Psychiatry Journal,* 6(9), 43-45.

Moss, Robert. (2004) *Dreamways of the Iroquois: Honoring the Secret Wishes of the Soul.* Rochester, Vermont. Inner Traditions/Destiny Books.

Nunn, John F. (1996) *Ancient Egyptian Medicine.* Norman, Oklahoma, University of Oklahoma Press.

Osmer, Bill. (2006) "Raga Chikitsa and Raga Ragini Vidya." Yogasangeeta.org/index. Accessed April 5, 2016.

Paxton, Frederick S. (1993) *A Medieval Latin Death Ritual: The Monastic Customaries of Bernard and Ulrich of Cluny,* St. Dunstan's Press, Missoula, MT.

Paxton, Frederick S. and Cochlin, Isabelle. (2013) *The Death Ritual at Cluny in the Central Middle Ages,* St. Brepols Publishers, Turnhout, Belgium.

Pratt, Christina. (2007) *Encyclopedia of Shamanism,* Vol. 1 Rosen Publishing Group.

Runningdeer, Islene. (1998) *Music as Medicine: Learning the Songs of the Self.* Burlington, Vermont. University of Vermont Press.

Schroeder-Sheker, Therese. (2001) *Transits: A Blessed Death in the Modern World,* St. Dunstan's Press, Fetzer Institute Monograph.

Smyth Babcock Matthews, William. (1891) *A Popular History of the Art of Music from the Earliest Times Until the Present.* Music Magazine Publishing Company. Chapter 1, "Music Among the Ancient Egyptians."

Swami Vishnudevananda. (1960) *The Complete Illustrated Book of Yoga.* New York, Bell Publishing Company.

Teeter, Emily & Johnson, Janet H. (2009) "Life of Meresamun: A Temple Singer in Ancient Egypt." *The Oriental Institute Museum Publications, No. 29,* University of Chicago Press (available online at OI.UChicago.edu).

BOOKS IN THE EVERY RIVER LIT SERIES

Series Editor: Lorene Shyba

A Wake in the Undertow: Rumble House Poems
Rich Théroux & Jessica Szabo
(2017)

Living in the Tall Grass: Poems of Reconciliation
Chief R. Stacey Laforme
(2018)

Vistas of the West: Poems and Visuals of Nature
Foreword: Doris Daley
Editors/Curators:
Lawrence Kapustka, Susan Kristoferson, Lorene Shyba
(2019)

Ducks Redux: Fueling Flames in Oil Land
LM Shyba and CD Evans
(2019)

Umbilicus: Poetry and Visuals of the Sensuous
Carrie Schiffler & Johanna Stickland
(2019)

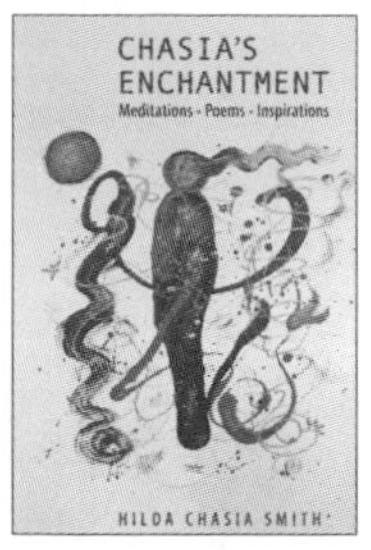

Chasia' Enchantment: Meditations, Poems, Inspirations
Hilda Chasia Smith
(2021)

The River Troll: A Story About Love in Color
Rich Théroux
(2021)

No Harm Done: Three Plays About Medical Conditions
Eugene Stickland
(2021)

The Little Book: Story Reader for a Free Ukraine
Mykola Matwijszuk
(1932, Reprinted with translation, 2022)

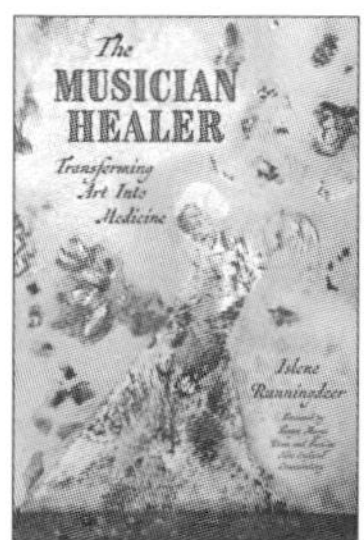

The Musician Healer: Transforming Art into Medicine
Islene Runningdeer
(2022)

UPCOMING

Olya & Lesya Escape the Invaders, Olya Illichov (2022)
Embrace Your Divine Plan, Julian Hobson, ed. (2023)

PHOTO: BRUCE FRAME

ISLENE RUNNINGDEER M.Ed.

Islene Runningdeer is a musician, therapist, educator, and writer who lives and works in central Vermont. She draws upon her French and Mi'kmaq/Abenaki First Nation roots to make music a joy. For more than forty years she has used music as a medicine to teach students about creative freedom and health, to aid and comfort patients and families during the dying process, to draw people with severe dementia out of their isolation and confusion, and to uplift and calm anyone within hearing, whether in church, the concert hall, the hospital, or the living room. Her work blends her lifelong interest in music of all kinds, psychology, physical health and spirituality. She is also the author of *Musical Encounters with Dying: Stories and Lessons.*